The
Birth
of
Jesus
Christ

COMPLETE NEW EDITION, THOROUGHLY REVISED.

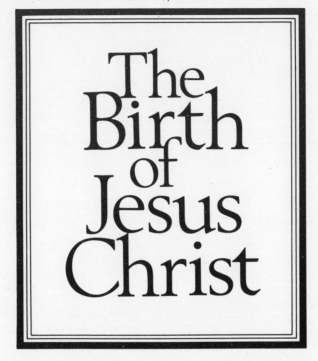

The Birth of Jesus Christ

THE APOSTOLIC FOUNDATION
OF THE
CHRISTIAN CHURCH

Volume Two

JOHN METCALFE

THE PUBLISHING TRUST
Church Road, Tylers Green, Penn, Buckinghamshire.

Printed and Published by
John Metcalfe Publishing Trust
Church Road, Tylers Green,
Penn, Buckinghamshire

—

First Published 1974
Reprinted 1980

Thoroughly Revised
Second Edition 1993

—

ISBN 1 870039 48 3. 2nd edition
(ISBN 0 9502515 5 0 1st edition)

—

Price 95p

CONTENTS

PART ONE

THE INCARNATION FROM MATTHEW

THE BIRTH OF JESUS CHRIST

PART ONE

THE INCARNATION FROM MATTHEW

> The book of the generation of Jesus Christ, the
> son of David, the son of Abraham.
>
> *Matthew 1:1*

MATTHEW recounts 'The generation of Jesus Christ the son of David, the son of Abraham' with the emphasis upon Jesus' humanity. And regarding his ancestry I observe that it is not merely a body from David or flesh from Abraham but of sonship from them. Their son by definition must possess not only a body but the life of their nature; their humanity is his generation and, asks the ancient prophet, Who shall declare it?

This genealogy in Matthew shows a human lineage, an ancestry of generated human life. Whatever is true of Jesus' divine sonship, this is true of his human ancestry, and Matthew in the first instance distinguishes and separates it from everything else—in the mystery of Messiah's person—in order to declare the generation of the humanity of one who is by nature the Son of man.

How wonderfully real is his humanity! How the unveiled glory of God shines in his countenance, yet conspires not to obscure but to enhance the touching humanity of the person who conveys it. Behold the Man! For the truth is that the body in which the Son of God became incarnate was of itself neither a mere shell nor a vacant frame: that which was Jesus' body—the body prepared—possessed intrinsic human life as such and was vital with inherent manhood. And although Jesus' body was the holy vessel of the divinity of the Son of God this does not lessen the truth that with the human frame the Son assumed that human nature proper to it by generation from David and Abraham.

Matthew proceeds with this revelation of the birth of Jesus Christ in a distinctive and orderly manner. Beginning at the genealogy, he continues with his account of the genesis of Mary's child by recounting what might properly be termed, *The Miraculous Conception*: for the origination of the humanity of Jesus Christ was unique and divine, not normal and human. The second thing illuminated indicates what may be referred to as, *The Mystic Union*: showing that with what was conceived in Mary was united the eternal Son of God, as taking human nature into union with himself in one person.

Finally because both these things unite in one, we must conclude that the former—the miraculous conception—took place not before but precisely parallel with the latter; and that the latter—and by this I mean the mystic union—was coincident with and not later than the former. Only thus is safeguarded the truth of the one person of Jesus Christ, notwithstanding uniting within himself the two real but distinct natures of deity and humanity.

Now to set this forth in order—that occurred in parallel—Matthew distinguishes carefully between things that differ and concentrates our attention upon them one at a time in sequence. Thus following upon the genealogy, he reveals how the holy child with this humanity from that human ancestry was conceived. A real son of true human nature is set forth in respect of his long and distinguished lineage and further declared in terms of his wondrous conception by the Holy Ghost in his mother Mary.

I

The Miraculous Conception

Now the birth of Jesus Christ was on this wise: When as his mother Mary was espoused to Joseph, before they came together, she was found with child of the Holy Ghost. Then Joseph her husband, being a just man, and not willing to make her a publick example, was minded to put her away privily. But while he thought on these things, behold, the angel of the Lord appeared unto him in a dream, saying, Joseph, thou son of David, fear not to take unto thee Mary thy wife: for that which is conceived in her is of the Holy Ghost.

Matthew 1:18-20

CAREFULLY notice that in this quotation there is as yet no direct exposition of the incarnation of the Son of God neither of the Word becoming flesh, nor yet of deity assuming humanity in union: that follows, but not till the truth of this passage is assimilated. First Matthew distinctly teaches the conception of Mary's child, handling the truth on this wise in order clearly to show precisely the nature of that humanity which the eternal Son took to himself, and exactly in which human frame the eternal Word was made flesh.

Matthew thus keeps us from the error of assuming that the Son in his humiliation merely 'wrapped himself in flesh', that the whole of the incarnation stood only in his taking a body.

It is true that the Son did 'wrap himself in our clay', that the incarnation did involve his taking the body prepared—but it is only half the truth, it is to know only in part. For it was not merely a body but human nature in a body, nor solely the flesh but also the humanity of this child of Mary, of that generation and conception: I say it was all of this that the Son of God took into union with himself in incarnation.

'She was found with child of the Holy Ghost.' It is upon this work of the Spirit that Matthew dwells for the time being; whatever else is true and much else also is true, and whatever happened besides at the same moment precisely and much else did so happen, still, to accommodate the limitations of our concentration in the unfolding of things above reason, perceived by faith, and declared through revelation, each one of the parallel occurrences is selected and separated in Matthew's doctrine—in due order—so that the mystery of Christ might be intelligibly comprehended in sequence not of occurrence but of narrative.

And first, declares Matthew, Mary was with child not by man—before they came together—but of the Holy Ghost. Note the divine person involved: it is not the Father nor yet the Son but it is the Spirit about whom Matthew is so precise, because he is at great pains to teach us the unique reality of the creation of Mary's baby, Mary's child begotten of the Holy Ghost.

It was the Holy Ghost that was active in respect of Mary's child; how and at what point the Son was active is another question dealt with elsewhere, as is also the work of the Father in respect of the incarnation. What Matthew is stressing in the first instance is that *it was the Holy Ghost that begat from the life and substance of Mary the child with which she was found.*

Hence it is enlarged upon a little lower: 'That which is conceived in her is of the Holy Ghost'. Again the emphasis:

Mary's child—of that lineage—was miraculously conceived without natural generation by supernatural creation; this, not by the Father whose activity at this time is not taught here: nor by the Son whose action at this moment is not now stated: but by the inworking and operation of the Spirit: here is the point of truth, that the conception of Jesus' humanity was from Mary by the Holy Ghost.

And the truth is that in the mystery of Jesus' person the conception of his sinless humanity is so important, so momentous, that upon this alone for the time being Matthew dwells that it may be distinguished beyond a peradventure. Then is plainly recognised what must be seen and held intelligently for salvation, in the belief of it: his true, real and impeccable human nature. Without believing this, one does not believe on the Lord Jesus Christ—nor can one! Hence Matthew declares his manhood at birth showing that this seed of the woman is really man, truly man, and lest we mistake—the Son of man! Of man, yes, but not by man, but by the Holy Ghost. Not naturally generated, but made of a woman.

Thus Matthew devotes these verses exclusively to revealing the conception in Mary by the creative work of the Holy Ghost of a real human child, having from her life and body a true human nature—Mary's child. The whole emphasis being to bring the unique, the miraculous, the awe-inspiring conception of that baby to the notice of the reader, and for the adoration of the believer.

How stupendous is what follows! How vastly staggering that the eternal deity in the person of the Son should take immediately into union by incarnation this human nature and frame thus conceived! Yet for all this superlative wonder, one is not to lose sight of the miracle of grace seen in the unique humanity of Jesus Christ the son of David, the son of Abraham in and of itself.

Consider this. His body is unique. It is conceived of the Holy Ghost and is therefore of course a holy thing; physically this frame was immaculate, the substance of it without inbred corruption, separate from sinners, spotless. The matter taken from Mary which comprised his unique body was utterly without that tainting presence of inbred sin with which the flesh natural to Mary was impregnated. For Mary's flesh was suffused—in common with mankind—with the humanly ineradicable presence of indwelling or original sin; original that is to Adam, from whom it was passed by natural generation to all posterity until this miraculous creation by the Holy Ghost of and from the seed of the woman.

His human nature is unique. This must follow. Although nonetheless a real man, he is another man. None was comparably conceived, except the first man Adam, the figure in innocence of him that was to come. The first man was directly created, which was not the case with any of his posterity. But now comes another man, a proper man, the second man, directly created—as to his humanity—not from the dust as Adam—who was of the earth earthy—but as it were from Eve the mother of all living: the seed of the woman is he, directly created from the womb of the virgin.

And hence we must call him not only The Second Man, I Corinthians 15:47, but also, verse 45, The Last Adam. For here is a humanity that is unique in its conception and here is a manhood intact in its integrity; faultless in its character, yet human in its nature.

This child was born of Mary, hung on his mother's breast, dandled on her knee; he was rocked in her arms, cradled in her bosom: he grew in wisdom and stature, was subject to his parents; he learned his trade, earned his keep, paid for his living; he hungered and ate, thirsted and drank, sorrowed and wept, tired and slept; he spoke and called, he cried and sighed, he breathed and spat.

We read of his body, hands, fingers, feet, eyes, head, legs, side, flesh, bones and blood. He was intelligent and thought, rational and willed, emotional and felt; he experienced joy and sorrow, was passionate and compassionate; he showed deep sympathy yet outraged indignation, touching forgiveness yet stern rectitude, human warmth yet profound spirituality; above all he loved and wanted love; he craved rational appreciation, emotional sympathy and mental understanding. Yet when all was told, the depths of his character, the profundity of his being, and the mystery of his person were beyond the comprehension of all mankind.

He prayed for himself, his work, and its success, with strong crying and tears; he feared God and was subject to discipline; he endured pain and hardship; he learned obedience by the things which he suffered. And he did suffer: in mind and heart, body and soul—he groaned in spirit—being at times sore troubled, even unto death; and indeed at the last he suffered to death. This is the man—behold the man!— that rose from the dead. This is the man of whom it is written that he liveth for evermore! This is the Second Man, and this is the Last Adam!

Now of this passage quoted from Matthew here is the sum: The miraculous conception of Mary's child has been revealed, and the doctrine is that without a father and contrary to the course of nature, by the extraordinary intervention of the authority of God—in this single case laying aside those laws that otherwise always govern mankind—without precedent and beyond subsequence, from the virgin's womb has been created a child by the Holy Ghost.

Now surprising as it may seem at first, so far nothing has been taught of the incarnation of the Son of God. The reason is not that he was not coincidentally active in incarnation, for his activity was precisely parallel with that of the Spirit. The reason is that it may be seen first and foremost in what flesh

8

the Son of God was incarnate, and which humanity it was that he took into union with himself. It is to clarify this that Matthew separates and distinguishes the work of the Holy Ghost to show the Spirit's creating from the substance of Mary's humanity—sin apart—that human nature and body prepared which the Son of God concurrently assumed into union with his deity in one person.

II

The Mystic Union

And she shall bring forth a son, and thou shalt
call his name JESUS: for he shall save his
people from their sins. Now all this was done, that
it might be fulfilled which was spoken of the Lord
by the prophet, saying, Behold, a virgin shall be
with child, and shall bring forth a son, and they
shall call his name Emmanuel, which being interpreted is, God with us.

Matthew 1:21-23

SUBSEQUENT in narrative but parallel in fact with the
preceding teaching (Mt. 1:18-20), Matthew proceeds in
the above quotation—verses 21-23—to unfold the truth by
revelation. However the revelation is given as by the breathing
of the Spirit, being rather by hint and gentle inference, than
by dictate and dogmatic utterance. But withal, there is no
room for question that the son now spoken of—and shall bring
forth a son—is he whose existence was before all worlds, whose
goings have been from everlasting.

The Son of God is now introduced in Matthew's record so
as to show beyond all reasonable doubt that the body and
human nature—conceived of the Holy Ghost in Mary—not
only never had but in any event never could have existence
as a separate entity of itself: it was created for nothing but the

instantaneous incarnation and the immediate assumption of the Son of God. At and with the creation by the Holy Ghost of that which was conceived in Mary, the divine Son received forthwith human nature into union with his own deity and took that frail and tiny substance that was to grow and be born into the world as his body, took it I say, as his own flesh.

In this way and in this way only, and at that point and that point alone, all the properties and life of human nature are assumed by him; yet that nature never having had *either the fusion of seed resulting from dual human parentage, or ever existence of itself by itself*, therefore on both counts there cannot possibly or remotely be predicated of it the entity of a separate human person. So that though the Son of God really has human nature in union with the divine, there is no duality, neither can there be, for he really is but one person, albeit in the mystery of that person his name—and no wonder—shall be called Wonderful!

By this declaration of the birth of Jesus Christ from the very beginning, we learn that he whose human nature and frame were at first referred to as the child with which Mary was found, and then as that conceived in her of the Holy Ghost, is now revealed to Joseph in a dream as 'a Son'. Assuredly not Joseph's son, but the virgin's child is from conception and by mystic union the Son of God, and was so declared well before his birth not only in primeval figure, nor solely by ancient prophecy, but now also through contemporary dream, confirmed and ratified by the event in due course.

Also to Joseph is revealed the name of the Son: thou shalt call his name Jesus. And just as the dream of his sonship hints his divinity, so also the whisper of his name infers his deity. Jesus! Thus is pronounced the Greek form of the Hebrew name Joshua, the ancient leader who brought God's people Israel dryshod over Jordan into the land of promise after the death of Moses.

However, Joshua of Hebrew fame was actually born with the name Hoshea—meaning salvation—and not till much later was he renamed Joshua by Moses, as though to show by the changing of his name that the salvation of God was not to be wrought by him, but by that promised Messiah whom Hoshea signified and typified in the authority of the new name given.

As to that new name, with Hoshea was interwoven the divine name Jehovah, a mystic union of the dual names of God and man bonded in the combined appellation Joshua, or as the English has it after the Greek form, Jesus; this signifying that he who should in the fulness of time save his people from their sins, must unite both deity and humanity in his own one person: which mystery was fulfilled in the birth of Jesus Christ the Son of God, being signified by his given name.

Moreover as in type with Israel under their Joshua so through Jesus Christ our Lord—who crossed the spiritual river of Jordan for us in death—the church has in a figure by Christ Jesus passed over dryshod already and furthermore is dead to the law by the body of Christ. For that old law of condemnatory commandments embodied in Moses was not only inadequate to bring Israel over to the promised land but even Moses himself was unable to cross on his own behalf!

Yet so marvellously effective was our Joshua that he crossed for himself—as witness the resurrection on the other side—and in crossing, vicariously brought over the whole church of God beyond the river of death. In so doing he took his people for ever beyond the sphere of legal condemnation, and so effectively removed the law from sight that the body of legal writ in Moses was not even found on its own side, the far side, Jordan! What a rest Jesus brings in! No wonder Satan contends it, and disputes about the body of Moses.

The ark also set forth Christ when Joshua commanded the priests to carry that ark down into Jordan, and remain with it poised over the now dry river bed till all Israel had filed across. This is seen fulfilled in Christ, typified by the ark of the covenant, when in the death of the cross his substitutionary humanity—the shittim wood—was offered and borne up upon the altar—the pure gold—of his everlasting deity, in the one priestly ark of his own person. This is the person who stood still for his people in the Jordan of death, whilst vicariously and in a mystery all that people passed before his face, seen as crucified with Christ: it was this work of God in such a death of so wonderful a person, that caused the very last one of the elect there and then to pass from death unto life, brought secure and safe to the other side.

So we learn that his name shall be called Jesus, for as Jehovah-Hoshea, in a mystic union, he unites both divine and human natures in one person. He is Joshua— Jehovah-Salvation. For what the ancient leader of Israel typified and depicted, he effects and concludes. His name shall be called Jesus, for this name alone combines the mystery of his deity and of his humanity in the unified perfection of his one person whilst at the same time indicating the everlasting efficacy of his saving work.

Only in the nature of his unique being could it follow that he should be the Saviour of his people. He alone on earth can save his people from their sins who hath a spotless humanity, an everlasting deity, yet is one person; he alone can remit sins who hath a divine title to do so, who is by appointment the one mediator between God and man, having both natures in his unique being; he alone, who answers to the ark of the covenant, who is in fact the priest for ever after the order of Melchisedec.

Such an one must of necessity be the perfect offering yet the true offerer: Jehovah God and yet substitutionary man; without sin yet made sin; he must in one person span infinity, contract eternity, and change immutability—no less his task!

13

He must magnify the law yet enlarge compassion; he must demand justice yet loose liberty; he must establish the heights of eternal righteousness yet move the depths of everlasting mercy—and so he came!

His is to plumb the unfathomable, effect the inconceivable, realise the impossible: and do so at once for ten thousand times ten thousand and thousands of thousands, in one poor substitutionary man-rejected God-forsaken broken body on the tree. His is to be hung naked between heaven and earth in the supernatural dark; his to be rejected of men, accursed by the law, and condemned of God. His is to fulfil the divine assignment from everlasting to be made sin at the appointed time outside Jerusalem: made sin in his nature as man who is God, yet was made sin by God. His is to conclude and ratify the ancient settlements of eternity as being the great bearer of the sins of his people there crucified upon the tree at Golgotha; yes, he shall of a truth save his people from their sins, and 'thou shalt call his name, Jesus.'

As to this mystic union being at the moment of conception, Matthew tells us that the creation by the Spirit of his humanity and body, the bringing in by the Holy Ghost of the seed of David from the womb of the virgin, the fulfilment of the dream of Joseph, all this was done to bring to pass the revelation that Jehovah—Emmanuel—would take into union with himself by assumption—as becoming incarnate—that human nature conceived of the Holy Ghost in Mary—that humanity. And would do so from the instant of creation, at conception, so that this humanity had no existence without such union, assumption and incarnation; yet withal so that it retained distinctly its integral humanity and intrinsic human nature.

All this was done so that the person of the eternal Son—who as proper to himself always possessed everlasting deity—might in a mystery take into union with his divine nature the created humanity thus prepared: so as to possess without confusion or duality of person, two distinct natures in one person: Jehovah-Jesus! Deity joined with humanity to bring in salvation. All this was done and done thus to fulfil the ancient prophecy of Isaiah quoted by Matthew, who peered back through the corridors of time, piercing the mists of ages past, to some seven hundred years before, discerning the realisation at last of the prophetic words dimmed with the long unfulfilled passage of some seven centuries.

Behold, saith Isaiah the prophet, a virgin shall be with child, and shall bring forth a son, and they shall call his name Immanuel, which being interpreted is, God with us. Notice the reference to a Child and a Son. It is the second time this has been stated. By ancient seer and modern dreamer God bears testimony: by the two witnesses of old covenant and new testament is the matter established: by Isaiah and Matthew, by apostle and angel, by God and man, in prophecy and vision.

In the certainty of this twofold witness hear the record: a child and a son! Matthew thus points out the simultaneous occurrence in fact, of what had been separated in sequence of narration for clarity of understanding: first of the creation by the Holy Ghost of the humanity of Mary's child—the term 'son' is here reserved for the divine relationship—then of the pre-existent divine Son's assumption of that humanity; a child —the reference in this place being exclusive to the human relationship—and a son: it is simultaneous in event.

This is confirmed by Isaiah 9:6, Unto us a child is born —answering to the first part of Matthew's doctrine, the conception by the Holy Ghost of Mary's child—Unto us a son is given—showing the pre-existent Son given in point of time at conception to take that humanity into union with himself. God with us, no less. Observe then that though the prophet forsees a born child made of a woman, a virgin, his piercing vision also perceives that the divine Son who is begotten and not made, whose going forth has been from everlasting, who

15

is the eternal, is in terms of his sonship not born but given: and given to be joined to that human nature created by the Holy Ghost from Mary, and that in the instant of its conception. In this way he is the gift of God. A child is conceived to be born and at conception the eternal pre-existent Son, given thus, takes that humanity into union with his deity in one person in mystic union: a child and a son.

For the Lord himself shall give you a sign, quoth Isaiah, Behold a virgin shall be with child and bear a son and shall call his name Immanuel. God with us! This signifies a great mystery: bone of our bone, flesh of our flesh yet very God of very God, Son of the Father. God with us, prophesied Isaiah, and if so not as he was with man in creation, neither as with the patriarchs of old, nor yet as he was with Israel in the old covenant: for that would deny the prophet's assertion that this was to be a future thing, a sign yet to come never before envisaged or realised.

God with us in a new and unique way, God with us in the sign of the virgin with child. For the sign itself is the virgin's conception, which Matthew carefully sets forth in order in the first instance; that sign, a virgin conceiving by the Holy Ghost, tells the watchful that the thing signified has come to pass. For the thing signified by the sign is that a Son is so given. Emmanuel is *thus* with us. At the moment the virgin is with child of the Holy Ghost, then comes to pass the signification of 'God with us'; for at that moment of conception the given Son takes that humanity into mystic union with himself.

Jeremiah writes of the sign on this wise: 'The LORD hath created a new thing in the earth, a woman shall compass a man.' That is, she shall conceive in her womb without the approach of man—much less being compassed by him—and carry within her in consequence a child who is neither of men nor by man yet hath true manhood! Still a virgin, nine full months she shall carry the manchild, conceived in the manner which the prophet expressly calls 'created'. This is that which the Holy Ghost wrought from within Mary; and thus is brought to pass the created new thing, A woman shall compass a man. Hence Isaiah's sign is Jeremiah's new thing.

From the very beginning of the conception itself Emmanuel assumed humanity in the tiny frailty of that which the Holy Ghost had created as fearfully and wonderfully made: 'Yea, in the belly thou knewest me.' It was not only that God in the person of the Son 'abhorred not the virgin's womb', but also, in an unfathomable mystery, in immeasurable condescension, from the moment of its existence united with himself that tiny, fragile, unborn infant nature. He was made flesh, he took upon him the body prepared, and in due course was born and called Jesus who should save his people from their sins. This is the sign; a sign to Israel in Isaiah, a sign to the Jews in Matthew, and—since it is interpreted—a sign to the Gentiles in grace.

Thanks be unto God. Amen.

PART TWO
THE INCARNATION FROM LUKE

PART TWO

THE INCARNATION FROM LUKE

L UKE informs us of that about which Matthew—in his especial emphasis on the doctrine—is silent: namely, of what was said by the angel to the virgin:

> And, behold, thou shalt conceive in thy womb, and bring forth a son, and shalt call his name JESUS.
>
> *Luke 1:31*

> Then said Mary unto the angel, How shall this be, seeing I know not a man? And the angel answered and said unto her, The Holy Ghost shall come upon thee, and the power of the Highest shall overshadow thee: therefore also that holy thing which shall be born of thee shall be called the Son of God.
>
> *Luke 1:34-35*

It was said to Mary, 'Thou shalt conceive in thy womb.' But what of the genesis, existence and formation of the seed of the woman before its actual development in readiness for that conception? For we assert that the seed thus conceived was *ever* without sin. If so, it follows of necessity that *before* the conception, in the very creation, development and formation of the seed as such in itself, as also in its passage from the point of origin *to* the womb—from its very inception—the seed had already been wonderfully prepared, and the Holy Ghost had already exerted his marvellous creative work under the overshadowing of the Almighty.

This is not to deny what has been asserted from Matthew— the instantaneous union and incarnation of the Son of God at and with conception: it is to declare the spotless purity in every way of that seed in its creation and development even before its conception was materially possible.

I assert it to be both proper and essential to observe that in the existence, development and passage of the seed thus passed to the womb for conception, one is to see already the marvellous work of God—for it is 'that holy thing' in and of itself. For this to be true then of necessity before conception and for it, the creative work of the Holy Ghost must have preceded so as to affect the two factors involved in the seed in and of itself: its material substance and its natural life.

Consider the first factor, the work of the Spirit of God in annulling and preventing the otherwise inevitable passage of inbred corruption in matter to that vital particle of the seed of the woman in which conception was to take place. Inbred corruption naturally exists in the very seed of both man and woman and it also increases commensurate with the growth of bodily substance after conception. The passage of it, by male seed and female, to all that is conceived and born of the flesh is true of all human nature for 'that which is born of the flesh is flesh'.

Hence David cries out under profound conviction as perceiving the root of the matter, 'Behold, I was shapen in iniquity; and in sin did my mother conceive me.' This was no moral question to David—not now a matter of what he had done, but of tracing why he had done it—when shapen, he had not been born: when conceived, he did not even exist in the sentient world; therefore this could only be true physically—not morally—of that tiny shapen seed.

There is an inbred corruption in the very matter of flesh, from whence arises degeneration, decay and death, besides the potentiality of disease, in the individual. This inbred sin in the flesh is even at birth stronger than the developing moral forces of the soul, as saith the psalmist in another place: 'The wicked are estranged from the womb.' This is before birth, thus before moral action. He continues, 'They go astray as soon as they be born.' That is from birth. So piteously and with such poignant sadness does David comment upon our own natural humanity. And so hath the honest man discovered at the root of the matter ever since: 'It is no more I that do it, but sin that dwelleth in me'; that which dwelt in him being stronger than he in whom it dwelt.

At the discovery of this profound truth, enlightened humanity is moved to cry in anguish and despair, Who shall deliver us from the body of this death? But the mercies of God are equal to the needs of man, and bring us glad tidings of great joy, for unto us is born a Saviour which is Christ the Lord. The heart of his salvation springs of love and it fulfils all righteousness, being expressed in substitution. Therefore we conclude that the perfect sinlessness of the Saviour's body is not only a requirement of his divinity who abhorred not the virgin's womb, but also of that very redemption which itself necessitates a spotless vicar in behalf of the defiled and guilty people.

Hence Jesus' conception was immaculate in the first instance because that flow of inbred sin from the first man which had spread its conquering sap through all flesh root and branch—and which was equally resident in the blessed virgin—had been divinely nullified. Because of this work of the Holy Ghost it was not in her impeccable seed thus passed to the womb. This seed, though in the likeness of sinful flesh, was in fact not sinful flesh itself, because of the overshadowing of the Most High and the inward working of the Holy Spirit of God.

In the second case neither was that intangible humanity—that maternal life—infusing the vital particle of matter subject to the bias natural to it because of its human origin. Mary's seed being seen not now as matter, flesh of her flesh, but as vitality, life of her life.

Albeit conception is not yet considered as taking place, before reaching the womb life of Mary's life lived in that seed in the very formation of its existence. Life which though not yet conceived, still was that which ordinarily in its very being would have been diffused with that bias and aberration contrary to and alien from the life of God: a depravity inherent not only in human matter but also in human nature.

For it was as true of the humanity of blessed Mary as of the holy apostle: 'The carnal *mind* is enmity against God: for *it* is not subject to the law of God, neither indeed can be.' The understanding being darkened, renewal is vital even in the spirit of the mind. The sensibility is likewise perverted, not only because of the lusts of the flesh, but also because of what the apostle calls, The blindness of their hearts. As says the Lord Jesus, From within, out of *the heart* of men, proceed evil thoughts, adulteries, fornications, murders. It is the moral heart that is itself warped, quite apart from any question of corruption in matter. The will too is concupiscent: 'For the good that I would I do not: but the evil which I would not, that I do.' In short, they that are in the flesh cannot please God, any more than can the flesh in which they are.

Therefore in the preparation of Mary's seed the work of God was twofold: materially in the matter of the flesh, and spiritually in the nature of the life. These two factors were involved in the seed of the woman which, when made ready, the Son of God was to assume in incarnation in the womb of the virgin.

Since it is called 'that holy thing', and in view of the divinity of the Son and further because of the necessity of perfection in the substitute, it follows that as to the life and matter of that seed the Holy Ghost had so creatively come upon Mary, that before conception, in every respect and both particulars, the essential feminine seed of potential humanity was impeccably perfect and without inherent corruption.

It is of this work of the Holy Ghost that the pre-existent Son of God prophesied—some one thousand years before coming into the world—in the following quotation from the Psalms, as interpreted in the epistle to the Hebrews: 'Wherefore he saith when he cometh into the world, A body *hast* thou prepared me.' That is, the seed of the woman was prepared *before* the coming of the Son into the world so as actually to be ready for him *when* he came. If so, then that seed was created by the Holy Ghost from Mary's life and substance so as to be without sin, and as prepared, then passed to the womb, being there suited for the Son's assumption of it into union with himself at the very moment of conception and incarnation.

The mystery itself is opened in answer to Mary's enquiry, *How shall this be seeing I know not a man?* It shall be by the threefold undertaking of God:

I

By the Authority of the Father

'The power of the Highest shall overshadow thee.'

Luke 1:35

IT was to be by the determinate counsel and foreknowledge of God the Father. From the depths of the riches both of the wisdom and knowledge of God proceeded these his unsearchable judgments, inscrutable ways and unfathomable counsels, according to the good pleasure of his own will thus abounding towards his Son, so as to purpose his advent in all wisdom and prudence.

I say, it shall be by this resolution of the deity from the ends of eternity, expressed in the Father's determination to bring to pass in point of time that which the Godhead from everlasting had conspired to effect: the tangibility of the intangible, the knowledge of the unknowable, the revelation of the impenetrable, the conception of the inconceivable, the incarnation of the deity, the humanity of the Son of God; the going forth out of eternity into time, out of the Godhead into humanity, out of heaven into the world, out of invisible spirit into visible form, out of the incomprehensible unknown into comprehensible knowledge—in a word the going forth from heaven of him whom the Father had sanctified and sent into the world in the fulness of time!

26

This was that for which time had waited: yea, the ages had trembled to usher in what came to pass with Mary. To the thoughtful it gives the only possible reason for the creation, the only conceivable coherence in the chaos, the only true light out of the darkness, the sole purpose to the apparent pointlessness. It was that which made Eve tremble, Sarah laugh, Rebecca depart, Rachel weep, Hannah whisper, Ruth entreat and Mary believe.

The Father directed the way of the Coming One about whom patriarchs had sighed, of whom prophets had hinted, for whom priests had substituted, by whom kings had reigned, and over whom the godly had yearned: the Messiah whose goings were from everlasting, whose promise was from creation and whose advent had come to pass in point of time.

Adam prefigured him, heaven held him, earth gasped for him, creation groaned for him, the creature travailed for him, humanity cried for him, Israel foretold him, the Isles waited for him, Joseph dreamed of him, the archangel announced him, John preceded him, the angels heralded him—but Mary bare him. Blessed art thou among women!

So the Father sent the Son. It was by his direction. The Galatian churches were instructed that when the fulness of time was come God sent forth his Son; it was the action of God and the Father. So also in the Roman epistle we are taught that God sent his own Son in the likeness of sinful flesh; God sent him, it was the direction of the Father that sent the Son when the chosen day arrived, and sent him in the likeness of humanity's external bodily form, not its internal conditional state. As also the Hebrews teaches us, in which Christ says in spirit when he cometh into the world, A body hast thou prepared me. It is prepared under the precise oversight of God and the Father, overshadowing the creative work of the Spirit, and directing the incarnation of the Son.

27

Further in answer to Mary's question, How shall this be seeing I know not a man? She was told by the angel Gabriel: 'therefore also that holy thing which shall be born of thee shall be called the Son of God.' Teaching us the second part of the threefold operation of God, the Son's assumption.

II

By the Assumption of the Son

'Therefore also that holy thing which shall be
born of thee shall be called the Son of God.'

Luke 1:35

THIS argues the pre-existence of the Son of God, and raises
the question, How long before he was made flesh and
assumed humanity in the body prepared was he pre-existent?
The answer is that he was self-existent: and if so, then eternal
and divine in his own nature, God withal, the I AM of eternity.

(i) The Pre-existence of his Person

Since creation is the divine prerogative, then the Son's
deity is clearly predicated by attributing the creation to him.
So John the apostle: 'In the beginning was the Word and the
Word was with God and the Word was God. The same was
in the beginning with God. All things were made by him and
without him was not anything made that was made.' This
clearly shows his deity as such and moreover his deity as
Creator, whose name is called 'The Word of God'.

Genesis 1:1 states categorically, 'In the beginning God
created the heaven and the earth', yet Hebrews 1:10 tells

specifically of the Son, by name, 'Thou, Lord, in the beginning hast laid the foundation of the earth; and the heavens are the works of thine hands', without doubt teaching that the Son is God himself: indeed stating in the previous verses: Unto the Son he saith, Thy throne, O God, is for ever and ever.

It is also true that within the singular unity of the Godhead these verses implicitly show the two Persons of the Father and the Son, One in the third Person of the Spirit—and thus reveal the most profound mystery of all—but beyond controversy they are explicit in demonstrating that the Son is the Creator, and that he is God. It could be to none other than God that these words apply which are spoken of Jesus in Hebrews 2, 'For whom are all things, and by whom are all things'; likewise John 1, 'He was in the world and the world was made by him'; for without doubt God made the world.

Hence where it is asserted that the Son—who was, before he came into the world—assumed the body prepared 'when he cometh into the world', it is clear that it is the Creator, God himself, that thus came. And so confirms Paul the apostle in the Colossians, speaking expressly of the Son, 'For by him were all things created, that are in heaven and that are in earth, visible and invisible.' But, 'In the beginning God created the heaven and the earth', Genesis 1:1. Not God created them by him: God created them; but says Paul, the Son created them: then the Son is God.

Not only is the Son declared to be the Creator—God himself —but his intrinsic divinity is seen in vision also in the old testament before his coming into the world. Surely the manifestation of the LORD to Abraham, Genesis 18, is to be seen as a vision of Christ: if not, who is he? For no man hath seen God at any time, but Abraham spoke face to face and said 'I have taken it upon me to speak unto the Lord; shall not the Judge of all the earth do right?' This being beyond dispute a visible manifestation of God to Abraham, and it

30

being past questioning that the only begotten Son is he who reveals him: then who else can this be? But if so, Son, Lord, and God are one and the same, and hence it was that Abraham rejoiced to see his day.

This is true also of Jacob who wrestled with the angel at Peniel, and said, 'I have seen God face to face, and my life is preserved.' But God dwelleth in light unapproachable, whom no man hath seen nor can see—then whom did Jacob see? The only begotten Son which is in the bosom of the Father he hath declared him. But Jacob called him, God. They who lack the sight may not, but Jacob saw for himself.

The brightness of God's glory and the express image of his person were wondrously envisaged in the Mount when Moses, Aaron, Nadab and Abihu, with seventy of the elders of Israel went up after both the book of the covenant and they themselves had been sprinkled with blood: 'And they saw the God of Israel: and there was under his feet as it were a paved work of a sapphire stone, and as it were the body of heaven for clearness.' But Jesus says to Israel, 'Ye have neither heard his voice at any time nor seen his shape.' Yet these Israelites at that time saw his shape down to the feet, and heard the voice of the God of Israel. Plainly therefore this is a vision of the Son, 'he hath declared him', and in the revelation he is distinctly called God.

Likewise an angel appeared to Manoah's wife—Judges 13— described as 'A man of God ... and his countenance was like the countenance of an angel of God, very terrible: but I asked him not whence he was, neither told he me his name.' As to that name, 'Why askest thou thus after my name seeing it is secret?' As then it was, but now is revealed by the coming of the Son into the world, for the angel is called: the angel of the LORD, a Man of God, a Man, an angel of God, the LORD, God. He is the One who went up on high after the sacrifice, and who else can this vision concern but Christ? Yet he is called God, even in visionary angelic appearance. Why then is his name kept secret? Because he was not then sent, but at that time only envisaged.

And this is true of the vision of Isaiah the prophet: 'I saw also the Lord sitting upon a throne, high and lifted up, and his train filled the temple. Above it stood the seraphims, and one cried unto another, and said, Holy, holy, holy, is the LORD of hosts: the whole earth is full of his glory. Also I heard the voice of the Lord, saying, Go, and tell this people, Hear ye indeed, but understand not; and see ye indeed, but perceive not. Make the heart of this people fat, and make their ears heavy, and shut their eyes; lest they see with their eyes, and hear with their ears, and understand with their heart, and convert, and be healed.'

This word was given to Isaiah when the vision of the glory of the LORD was revealed, and in the book it appears to be a reference to the prophet's contemporary ministry. But this is not the case in fact, for in the new testament John assures us that both the vision and the speech are in fact really a revealed sight and a prophetic utterance of Christ. The words are a prophecy concerning the effect upon the Jews of the person and the public ministry not of Isaiah but of Jesus: 'That the saying of Esaias the prophet might be fulfilled', John 12:37-40. This shows indisputably that Esaias 'the prophet' foretold of Jesus, saw him and spake of him and his ministry.

Moreover in John 12:39 the apostle John states categorically of Jesus' ministry, 'Therefore they—*the Jews*—could not believe —*in Christ*—because that Esaias said again—*in Isaiah 6, immediately after the vision of the LORD of hosts*—'He hath blinded their eyes, and hardened their heart; that they should not see with their eyes, nor understand with their heart, and be converted, and I should heal them'; plainly teaching that these words concern *Jesus'* person and ministry, not Isaiah's.

32

Then John straightway informs us: 'These things said Esaias when he saw his glory and spake of him', John 12:41. Saw whose glory? Without doubt, the glory of God, the LORD of hosts. Spake of whom? Truly, of him whose glory Isaiah had just seen, that is, of Jehovah. Yet that speech of Esaias was applied expressly to Jesus' person and ministry by John in the preceding verses: it is *he* of whom Isaiah spoke. And since the one of whom Isaiah prophetically spake these words is the same one as he whose glory Esaias saw—'*saw* his glory and *spake* of him'—therefore it follows beyond question that Jesus and the LORD of hosts seen in glorious vision are one and the same, demonstrating both the Son's pre-existence and deity.

Neither can it be doubted that Daniel's manifestation of the 'Ancient of Days' finds an answer in John's vision of the Lord Jesus Christ, the Son of man, whose 'Head and hairs were white like wool, white as snow', giving the impression of ancient days beyond measure, of the Eternal. Further, Daniel's Ancient of Days was clothed in a garment white as snow, and John's Son of man was 'Clothed in a garment down to the foot', the impression of which was radiant.

And that vision which struck Daniel dumb was of 'A face as the appearance of lightning, and his eyes as lamps of fire, his feet like in colour to polished brass.' Whereas the risen Son of man appeared centuries later as one whose 'Countenance was as the sun shineth in his strength; his eyes were as a flame of fire, his feet like unto fine brass.' Who can possibly doubt the pre-existence of the Son when Daniel envisaged before he came into the world what John saw after he had departed from it? His life was as eternal before assumption, as it is perpetual after resurrection, and hence it is written, Jesus Christ the same yesterday, and today and for ever.

The Son is seen as Creator then; moreover the visions of the old testament before his advent show his pre-existence and deity. Not only so but the many types and figures under the old covenant clearly affirm the divinity of the Son of God. For example take Jacob's ladder, seen in the dream recorded in Genesis 28. 'And Jacob dreamed, and behold a ladder set up on the earth, and the top of it reached to heaven.' What does this mean but that the ancient plea, 'Oh that I knew where I might find him!'—had now been answered? *The top of it reached to heaven!*

Thus the anguished cry of the smitten man, 'Neither is there any Daysman betwixt us, that might lay his hand upon us both'—has been met in a ladder which indicates one Mediator between God and man which brings both together, uniting them in its own existence; or rather, pre-existence.

This ladder scales the celestial heights, plummets the terrestrial depths, spans the yawning gulf, arches over infinity, and forms a way between the remotest and most alienated realms in being—heaven and earth—bringing together in its integral span both creature and Creator. It *is* the way to heaven! I am the Way, saith Jesus, no man cometh unto the Father but by me. It reaches in its nature to all that is in heaven, and descends in its compass to all that is on earth, unifying both together in its intrinsic being. Said the one who stood on earth, 'No man hath ascended up to heaven, but he that came down from heaven, even the Son of man which is in heaven.'

'And behold, the angels of God ascending and descending on it.' This teaches by Jacob's dream that not only had the way of access been revealed, but that it was even then effectual for immediate and constant communication, bringing in a responsive union. A communion is achieved in which heaven corresponds with earth, and earth answers by way of angelic messengers. Here is the antitype: 'Jesus said, Verily, verily, I say unto you, Hereafter ye shall see heaven open, and the angels of God ascending and descending upon the Son of man.' There is Jacob's ladder. If it be enquired, How does this show the eternity and deity of the Son of God? I reply, because he is himself the answer to this figure, being able to achieve in his own person and by his personal work what that dream demonstrates. Whence eternal divinity, incarnate humanity, and the union of both in one without confusion follow of course, being of necessity prerequisite for all that the vision unveils and foreshadows.

'And behold, the LORD stood above it, and spake.' Yea, and such the efficacy of this ladder, the man slept below it, and heard! The elect man at the foot of the ladder prefigures the singular seed of Abraham in whom all nations should be blessed. This is the divine Son that came down from so high above in heaven, and by perfection in Manhood in the world so far below displayed the fulness of what was in the highest, upon the earth. From the opened heaven above the Father spake of the Man in Israel beneath: 'This is my beloved Son in whom I am well pleased.'

Therefore it is in his manhood alone that God is made known, and known as the Father above through the Son below, by a way between in the Spirit withal. Hence it must be of necessity that the Man beneath is God manifest in the flesh, for whoever saw him saw the Father: 'behold the LORD stood above it!' The life was thus manifested, the apostles heard the Word made flesh, saw him with their eyes who came from heaven, looked upon God and lived, their hands handling the Word of life.

They bare witness, they show unto us that Eternal Life, which was—*was* mark it, *was* eternally—with the Father, and if eternally with the *Father*, then, *as Son*. Eternally as Son. This was manifested unto the apostles: 'us'. If this be not the incarnate Son in the person of Jesus, the seed of Abraham, the Eternal Son, the Man at the foot of the ladder, then who is this Eternal Life, how was he with the Father eternally, whence came he, for what reason, and how saw they him?

35

That the top of the ladder reached to God in heaven shows that if God is brought to men in Man by its descent, men are brought to God in the Son by its ascent. Were not the Son eternally divine, then this picture—that the top of the ladder reached to God in heaven—would have no meaning. For it is axiomatic that just as in reaching to man from God perfect manhood is necessary, so also in reaching to God from men absolute divinity is essential. Otherwise the reach were inadequate—but the dream shows that it is adequate: the top of it *reached* to heaven!

For if on the one hand the incarnation showed the manhood of the pre-existent Son, 'Verily he took not on him the nature of angels'—because such angelic nature could not reach to man—so on the other, to reach effectually from true manhood to God, he who became incarnate could not possess less than that absolute deity proper to the divine Person.

Likewise the ark in the old testament set forth the deity of Christ and therefore necessarily his pre-existence. Hebrews 9 tells us that in the Holiest of All beyond the veil, there was 'The ark of the covenant overlaid round about with gold, and over it the cherubims of glory shadowing the mercy seat.' That this was manifestly a type of Christ is clear in that the same word translated 'mercy seat' in Hebrews— ἱλαστήριον — expressly refers to the Son of God when translated 'propitiation' in Romans 3:25, 'Christ Jesus, whom God hath set forth a propitiation.' Showing beyond dispute that in the Propitiatory or Mercy Seat is seen a figure of Christ together with the ark of which it was an integral part. And this John confirms using another form of the same word— ἱλασμός —'And he'— he, mark it, Jesus Christ—'*is* the propitiation.'

Why then do the ark and the mercy seat prefigure Christ, and in what way does this demonstrate his pre-existence and deity? I answer, much every way, but to the present purpose chiefly as regards the substances from which the ark was made. Exodus 25 tells us that the ark was made of shittim wood in the form of an open chest, that it was overlaid with pure gold, and within it the two tables of stone were laid, the ark then being closed over by the propitiatory cover made wholly of gold all of one piece with the cherubim.

Two different substances from two distinct—nay, opposite—realms, were fused together in one distinctive union. The first, gold, being mineral. The second, wood, being in its nature vegetable. The one formed over countless aeons, profoundly precious, mined from the soaring cloud-wreathed mountains of God, as it were eternal in the heavens, one with and in the rock, a mineral immutable and priceless, reflective of all that is changeless and perpetual, subject neither to time nor decay. The other not mineral at all, being humble timber, of short and mutable span, of transient life subject to its limited age and curtailed by its own natural decay, rooted in and growing from the lowly soil, dependent on sun and water for life, of comparatively little intrinsic value, and formed in its being by nothing more than the annual growth of its own earthly substance.

So in Christ—and indisputably the ark is a type of Christ—God and man, heaven and earth, are brought together in one. The express manifestation of God in the tabernacle is without doubt depicted by pure gold: it is God revealed, the visible reflection of the glorious deity, the brightness of his glory. Extraordinary, that this should be overlaid upon so weak, poor and inexpensive a substance as wood! But not if it be considered in terms of the humanity which the glorious Son of God took upon himself: who was in the form of God, who thought it not robbery to be equal with God—pure gold!—yet who made himself of no reputation, and took upon him the form of a servant, and was made in the likeness of men—shittim wood! Yes, in the sinless likeness of sinful flesh. This is what Paul calls the weakness of God, but it is stronger than men, and bears uniquely and distinctively the weight of his eternal glory—absolute deity—whilst containing the union of both within the integrity of his own being.

If it is not so, why is the ark thus? Why do the apostles say, this *is* Christ? Clearly, because it is of two distinctive substances in one ark, as also because it has its own unique position, its own specific dimensions, its own hidden contents, and its own significant testimony; these things being innate in its construction; moreover it is: 'There I will meet with thee, and I will commune with thee.'

But we have yet further witness to the pre-existence of the Son, for the Patriarchs also owned the deity of Christ. For example, Abraham in his own lifetime rejoiced to see Christ's day and, we are told, actually saw it, and was glad. Contrariwise, thousands of years later, the Jewish descendants of that patriarch treated Christ abominably when he told them the truth which he had heard of God, and, said Jesus, 'This did not Abraham'. What did not Abraham? Abraham did not treat Christ abominably when *in Abraham's lifetime,* he, the Son, told that patriarch the truth. For this verse, John 8:40, to have any meaning at all, it follows that just as really as then in the body Jesus taught the Jews, so also thousands of years previously in spirit the pre-existent Son likewise had taught their ancestor Abraham.

It does not surprise us therefore to read Christ's assertion, 'Before Abraham was, I am'; this as to pre-existence. As to self-existent deity, I AM and Jehovah are synonymous: 'God said unto Moses, I AM THAT I AM: and he said, Thus shalt thou say unto the children of Israel, I AM hath sent me unto you, the LORD God of your fathers, the God of Abraham, the God of Isaac, and the God of Jacob.' But, before Abraham was, I AM, said Jesus, and seven times over asserted the same.

The Prophets likewise honoured the Son even as they honoured the Father, saying unto Zion of Christ 'Behold your God!' And who other than the LORD, suddenly come to the temple of his body, could bear the divine names by which he should be called: Immanuel; God with us; the Son given; the

Wonderful; the Counsellor; the Mighty God; the Everlasting Father; the Prince of Peace; Jehovah's Fellow; The Lord our Righteousness?

Further—though examples might be multiplied beyond measure—Micah tells of the place of his birth: 'But thou, Bethlehem Ephratah, out of thee shall he come forth unto me that is to be ruler in Israel; whose goings forth have been from of old, from everlasting.' But who could possibly go from everlasting unless he were eternal? It is not here asserted that he went into eternity, but that he comes out of everlasting! To where? To be born in time as man at Bethlehem. Then the babe of Bethlehem is the High and Lofty One that inhabiteth Eternity whose name is Holy, as his nature is divine, his being everlasting, and his Sonship eternal.

The wise man also assures us of the Wisdom of God, otherwise known as the Logos, reason, or word, 'The LORD possessed me in the beginning, before his works of old; I was set up from everlasting.' By which we learn that God's wisdom or truth is personified, as also Jesus taught: I AM the truth. Then it follows he was pre-existent so as to be before the creation, even from everlasting, and, if so, the eternal God, divine withal, possessed of glory with and equal to the Father as Son or ever the world was. It is this Word, or Wisdom, that was made flesh, the Life—that eternal Life—that was manifested.

The kings owned him King of kings and Lord of lords also. King David calls Christ, Lord, saying: 'The LORD said unto my Lord.' If David called Christ, Lord, then how is he his son? I answer, by right of inheritance through promise, and by the seed of the woman in fact; but not by fatherhood in nature, for Christ is the Son of God in deity, born of the virgin in time, and pre-existent from eternity. Hence David does obeisance, calling him Lord in the past tense some one thousand years before his birth. And such kings are no less than prudent, for not only is he the Prince of the kings of the earth but, 'The Lord at thy right hand shall strike through kings in the day of his wrath'!

Priests also owned the One Mediator between God and man, that Daysman—Job 9:33—who singularly and uniquely possesses the nature of both in One Person. For from the ancient times the Levitical priests in Abraham payed tithes to the everlasting Son who abode a priest continually. For Christ is a priest *for ever* after the order of Melchizedek, and these words mean not only his perpetual continuance henceforth, but also his eternal pre-existence hitherto: without father, without mother, without descent, having no beginning of days, he abideth continually. His is an endless life, not only in forthcoming eternity, but from everlasting ages: the Eternal, not simply the Immortal. And, if so, as Son. 'Unto the Son he saith, Thou art.'

God the Father testifies to the equal deity of the Son—who himself thought it not robbery to be equal with God, for he and his Father are One—by sharing his name and divine prerogatives as with Jehovah's Fellow. Hence the I AM of Exodus 3:14 is the I AM of John 8:58. That worship which only God may receive, Isaiah 45:23—'Unto *me* every knee shall bow, and every tongue shall swear'—is given to the Son: Phil. 2:10-11, 'At the name of *Jesus* every knee shall bow, and every tongue confess'. It is to the glory of God the Father that the Son should be honoured in deity even as the Father himself.

So, naturally, divine prerogatives are equally shared. None can forgive sins but God only, yet the Son forgives them, and that on earth. As also the Son creates, sustains the universe, shapes time, quickens whom he will, raises the dead, judges the world, ushers in the world to come, is called King of kings and Lord of lords, the Lord of glory, the King of glory, and the Lord of hosts withal. These names are doubtless synonymous with the sole prerogatives of JEHOVAH, declaring a glory which he will not give to another, yet which he shares equally with the only begotten who is the brightness of that glory, and who is the express image of the divine Person.

The history of the people of God also shows the Son's pre-existent deity, through the repetition by Jesus himself on earth of Jehovah's unique divine activity from heaven, so many long ages before: but if so, it must be the same divine person active in both cases. For example, the children of Israel received drink in the wilderness from Jehovah. Yet Jesus cried, If any man thirst, let him come unto me and drink. But since these two events are separated by an age, the perpetuity of the Son follows of course.

Again, it was God himself who gave the people manna in the wilderness, as it is written 'He gave them bread from heaven to eat.' Yet millennia later Christ declares that the bread of God is he which came down from heaven: 'I am that bread.' And as if that were not enough to show that he is timeless in his being and self-existent in his deity, notice that what the arm of Jehovah did in giving bread from heaven as manna to the multitude, Jesus does on earth by feeding first five thousand and then four thousand souls. Clearly showing that Jehovah and Jesus are one and the same.

No wonder that John the Baptist, the last of the great succession of Hebrew prophets and the contemporary of Jesus, should discern in that heavenly Man the Son's eternity, and say: 'After me cometh a man which is preferred before me: for he was before me'; yet not before by birth, for John was the elder by six months: but by divine nature, for the pre-existent Son who assumed humanity was not only before John but before Abraham, too. Yea, 'From everlasting to everlasting thou art God.'

Hence he receives worship, which thing would be idolatry were he not God in his own person, for, 'Thou shalt worship the Lord thy God and him only shalt thou serve.' But saith God of the Son, 'Let all the angels of God worship him'—

angels, mark it—moreover, ten thousand times ten thousand and thousands of thousands of angels worship the Lamb, and besides, the four and twenty elders fall down and worship the Lion of the tribe of Judah, the Root of David. 'I AM the LORD thy God which brought thee up out of the land of Egypt, Thou shalt have no other gods before me; thou shalt not bow down thyself to them nor worship them.' But angels and men bow down to the Son, worshipping him with the worship that is due to God alone.

What myriads, what a great multitude of the redeemed from among men—so great that no man is able to number them—behold God and the Lamb upon the same throne, give equal worship, ascribe the same praise: and with all angels, every creature, all creation, fall down on their faces before the throne, prostrate in worship before God and the Lamb. And why not? For he is thy Lord, and worship thou him.

(ii) *The Knowledge of the Deity*

So it is the truth, and the truth revealed in the Son, that he and his Father are one. Eternally one. Equally it is true that the Holy Ghost proceeds from the Father, and is given by the Son, and that the Father, the Son, and the Holy Ghost, are one: one God in three Persons, three Persons in one God. This unity is the most profound of all mysteries, and impossible to receive rightly, save by revelation. This is that unity which is made manifest in him who, though in the form of God, and equal with God, made himself of no reputation, taking upon himself the form of a servant, being made in the likeness of men, found in fashion as a man, yet, withal, being God manifest in the flesh.

Despite that as man in the place of Surety and Mediator the Son ascribes deity to God and the Father, there never was, is, or can be any detraction from his own equal, eternal, pre-existent and essential divinity in person, only a wondrous manifestation of condescending grace to lost sinners, so as to act as their Saviour in substitutionary manhood, and reveal the Deity in divine Fatherhood.

From this it follows that the intrinsic and personal deity of the incarnate Son is not that which he came publicly to display —though it could not be hid; indeed it was that without which the revelation of God and the Father could not be conveyed —nor is it that of the Holy Ghost: it is the *Father's* deity that the divine Son wonderfully manifests in Manhood. He that hath seen me hath seen the Father: I and my Father are one. Hence, no man knoweth the Son but the Father, neither knoweth any man the Father save the Son, and he to whom the Son will reveal him.

Theologians, divinity doctors, the clergy, may try by reason and philosophy, tradition and learning, to understand and explain divine relationships, but all they can do is confound their historical confusion worse confounded. The world by wisdom knew not God, and no subsequent learned cleric shall rectify the error. Here is the hidden wisdom, revealed immediately by the Spirit within, shining into the heart of the poor in spirit—who are chosen to receive it—teaching by experience, by heart-union, the mystic intimacy of divine relationships in one God. As Mary concluded, The rich he hath sent empty away.

This truth—not only of the relationships between Father, Son and Holy Ghost in one God, but also of how the spiritual knowledge of God is conveyed—shall ever stand. It shall never be prized open by human intellect nor explored by carnal reason, any more than it can ever be attained by natural logic or religious study. Man in his proud pretension may attempt this divine work, but the resultant dry, dark and arid confusion shall be made clear to all. These things are known solely by revelation, in the spiritual experience of them; and so says the apostle Paul: it is by the revelation of the mystery.

Though multitudes have viewed Jesus Christ—and their successors still imagine him—in a form which they conclude from external sight or textual appearance, they all stumble upon the dark mountains of that presumptuous pride which supposes adequacy within oneself to grasp the mystery of his Name. They attempt to lay hands upon him by intellectual conclusion from scripture, or sentimental sensation from drama, or else from the withered arm of human will by works: such as these know nothing in reality!

For it is ever true that 'No man knoweth the Son but the Father'; and, 'every man that hath heard and hath learned of the Father cometh unto me.' Moreover 'God hath revealed these things unto us by his Spirit'; and, 'as many as are led by the Spirit of God they are the sons of God.' It must be inwardly and spiritually that those led by the Spirit discover Christ himself, in person, solely through interior revelation from the Father. Neither dare they proceed beyond what is actually revealed to them personally, saying, 'I know not; one thing I know, that, whereas I was blind, now I see'; and see to the confusion of the learned doctors of the law, the haughty scribes of the letter, and the disdainful priests of the hierarchy.

So concludes David in Psalm 131, saying, LORD, my heart is not haughty, nor mine eyes lofty: neither do I exercise myself in great matters, or in things too high for me. Surely I have behaved and quieted myself, as a child that is weaned of his mother: my soul is even as a weaned child. Let Israel hope in the LORD from henceforth and for ever.

This from the psalmist who had received such astonishing insights as are manifest for example in the 110th Psalm, the 22nd Psalm, the 16th Psalm, or the 32nd Psalm. This! From the sweet psalmist of Israel whose gaze pierced heaven, saw the LORD, discerned mysteries, penetrated the future, saw things to come, and foretold the revelation of the mystery of Christ.

If so, how can such a man utter the paradox of Psalm 131? Because all that he perceived and discerned was by direct revelation from the Holy Ghost, by the voice of God to his own soul, not of men, neither by man, but by the Lord, even the LORD his God. Nor yet was his profound insight through his own brains, gifts, education, study, or religious works—or that of others—but solely from the Spirit of the Lord.

Hence David's meaning in Psalm 131 is this: he will look and wait for nothing but the teaching of God's Spirit. He will eschew the endeavour, logic, reasoning, prying, and effort of his own mind; he will proceed ever and only upon a basis of utter self-distrust and total self-judgment, so as to be wholly dependent upon and stayed up by the inward and spiritual teaching of the Holy Ghost. Wonderful teaching! That which came to the consciousness of his interior soul by revelation made known in mystery, all to magnify and glorify Christ, and all proceeding from the sheer grace and sovereign will of God and the Father whom David had not chosen, but who had chosen David.

And all who would know the Lord in truth must heed David's example, for it is to this heart-attitude of humility that the knowledge of the Son is given. This is especially true concerning the mystery of Christ's person and the revelation of Father, Son, and Holy Ghost. Here in particular there must be an heartfelt self-abasement on the one hand, and a being led of the Holy Ghost on the other. Here especially one must avoid men's teaching, one's own conjectures, mere human reasoning, but contrariwise stay under the revelation of the Spirit within holy writ, under the sent ministry of that doctrine which sounds within as when 'deep calleth unto deep at the noise of thy waterspouts'.

Humility alone might have taught men caution as regards the knowledge of the Son of God, in that whilst many scriptures patently reveal his intrinsic deity, others go further and show his divine relationships in one God with the Father and the Spirit. Yet notwithstanding these passages, another whole body of texts reveals the Son's humanity, with varied, full, and touching references to Jesus' confidences, prayers and cries to his God and Father. But also, many other places teach the union of his deity and his humanity without confusion of nature in one person. This again being extended to those scriptures which reveal his deity in his humanity, his humanity in his deity, yet which distinctively safeguard the integrity of each nature in one person.

Not to mention the references to the varied qualities of his divine character so often outshining, nor to refer to the many passages speaking of the attributes of his human nature so marvellously made manifest. Still less is it to speak of his distinctive relations to Israel, his further offices for the whole world, or the profound mysteries of his indissoluble union with the elect. And amazing as it is to see the depth and scope indicated already, this is not yet to mention the tremendous doctrines by which the Spirit brings to light his wonderful and complex work.

I say, would not humility itself teach—seeing so great a volume of material, so vast a range covered, and so profound a depth sounded; seeing that such weighty, divine and heavenly matter is here presented, I ask, would not humility itself teach men—that which David expressed in the 131st Psalm? With such a subject as the Son of God, does not modesty demand in man what made the seraphim cover their faces? With such a body of truth concerning Christ's person to be found in holy writ, what mere man is sufficient for these things? Who shall rightly divide the word of truth for us, properly discriminate the various shades of meaning, with meetness distinguish between things that differ, laying down the doctrine in order and in the right proportion, as well as in its proper place—who?

With man it is impossible, and yet strangely never were men more impudently presumptuous, nor arrogantly forward, than in rushing into the work of the ministry, proclaiming themselves to be teachers of all, and finally substituting an entire meagre and shrivelled system of their own devised notions in place of that ministry of the Holy Ghost which brought in the spiritual and original simplicity which was in Christ!

But as it was with the prophets in Israel, so it was with Jesus and the Jews; as it occurred in the apostles' days with the false claims of the deceitful workers, thus it shall be to the end. Observe what a seed-bed for every vile growth of miserable conceit is that knowing pride of religious man—who will force himself into 'full time service'—there to display that hypocritical imitation which cannot keep its working hands from fingering the things of God, but must perforce thrust itself into the sanctuary—presuming to support the entire work of God with the defiled and iniquitous arm of the flesh.

Precisely because of the greatness of the Son—necessitating such a wealth of widely ranging truth, and so great a depth of matter at each point in that range—there is endless possibility for confusion by the self-willed, ignorant, opinionated, and for those who seek the distinction of being purveyors of so-called new truths.

And not without much-vaunted sincerity! For presumptuous men soon reduce the doctrine of Christ to that tiny fragment which is all that they apprehend of it. Next even this they quickly diminish to what is personal to their own conceit, and hence they trumpet so strongly about it! And thus there comes to pass again that which was true in the days of the Judges: Every man does that which is *right* in his own eyes. But, 'I command thee this day to do that which is right in the eyes of the LORD thy God.'

From pretentious pride many run before they are sent—if they are sent at all—and, ill-prepared or half-prepared, one will see the teaching and necessity of Christ's deity, but will diminish his manhood. Another his manhood and derogate his deity. Yet others profess divine relationships yet deny their nature. These with the mouth profess to hold the deity of the Son, yet in reality impugn his divinity by denying that the relationship of Son with the Father ever subsisted from all eternity, asserting that this was a relationship assumed from the incarnation. Oh: pernicious heretics! Where is discernment, that such things ever gain a hearing?

The truth is that—along with so many errors—such heretics gain an entrance and footing with the people by depending upon justified attacks on theology and theologians, whose invention of office and confusion of doctrine is so very obvious as against the humility and clarity which was in Christ. Such attacks pour scorn upon academic and scholastic language which is—it must be admitted—totally alien to the words which the Holy Ghost useth. Such level against the many serious and not so serious faults in traditional and historical schemes, enshrined and perpetuated in the various institutions, confessions, and creeds, of so-called religious learning, themselves absolutely contrary to apostolic tradition and clean outside the actual church itself.

This polemical warfare feeds and thrives upon obvious ignorance—as well as the covering up of that ignorance by mutual consent—on the part of ecclesiastically endorsed commentators who are conspicuous for little except their ability to bore their readers to tears when they hold forth on those passages clear to everyone, and amaze them with irrelevant brevity in places where difficulty really exists. Errors soon gain credence when the sense of justice in the people is offended, and when it is pointed out how obvious is the refusal of hierarchical clericalism—in times past and present—to conform to the humbling simplicity and spiritual verity which is so manifest in Jesus Christ—all this! What a ground it lays for every novel error.

And again, so many errors gain credence with the simple because of the great and diverse display of what are in fact totally irrelevant scriptural texts. But to the simple, it looks impressive. And in particular the vast mass of references to the person of Christ in holy writ lends itself so easily to their being mishandled by heretics.

With so fine and spiritual a divinity needed properly to discern the use, place and proportion of the doctrine, how easy it becomes for false apostles, deceitful workers, unsent ministers, or even sincere zealots to fill up their error with the froth of fervent professions and sentimental flattery, poured out over the one whom they call 'Jesus', to the admiration of their ignorant followers. Having done that, what remains for them but to wind around the heart of their deception the diverse strands of irrelevant bible references, till it becomes well nigh indistinguishable either for what it really is, or even for what might be remotely suspect by the general mass of the people.

From this, it is not surprising that—given a winding and weaving of biblical texts—many errors can gain and have gained credence with the simple. So it is with the error concerning the eternal relationship of the Son with the Father—those who pretend to hold the Son's pre-existence in deity, but deny it to him in the Name of Son or in terms of Sonship. It will be found that the advocates of this error hold forth with texts on the incarnation, assumption, purpose, manhood, work and mediatorial glory of the Son of God, and the meanwhile will quite accurately—and rightly—snipe at the crumbling façade of traditional clerical fabrications.

But the method of propagating error remains the same; when all is said and done, these superfluous texts—having nothing whatever to do with opening up the nature of the eternal relations of the Father and the Son—prove nothing more than the necessity of bolstering weakly argued error with irrelevant and misapplied scripture, and that to deflect the eyes of the unwary from the slyness of the argument.

Further, since many of the old theological creeds and pontifications, hallowed by long Catholic tradition, are nothing but badly worded fiats based on references which really have no bearing at all on the subject, it is quite easy for the erroneous triumphantly to show that many scriptures do not at all teach what slaves to tradition have blindly accepted as their meaning.

The truth is that what the erroneous accuse traditional clericalism of doing, in another way they themselves have done: they have pried into what is not revealed and attempted to explain what is not explicable. And where divine relationships are but stated, they could not leave alone such high and holy things in the spirit of the meek acceptance seen in David in the 131st Psalm, no, in their turn they themselves had to meddle with what is utterly beyond that which is revealed.

They could not rest with justly rebuking the impositions of Roman Catholic and following Protestant theologians, who impudently philosophised and scholastically speculated beyond all that is written to set forth eternal relationships in Deity—where were theologians when God laid the foundations of the earth, since they are so wise above what is written?—no, having rebuked, they could not rest, but must blunder into the pit of which they themselves had given warning. And because the Spirit's voice on so exalted, holy, and divine a matter is so hushed, so faint, such a whisper, so still, so small, they in their rushing, headlong quest for new light missed it, and fell, to be taken in that which they digged for others.

(iii) *The Eternity of his Sonship*

The error under consideration is that heresy which asserts three unknown and unnamed divine persons in the Godhead, having no revealed relationships in deity, who *assumed the names and relationships* of Father, Son and Holy Ghost *at the incarnation* in order to effect redemption. No such relationships are considered as having been in existence prior to the incarnation. But we assert the eternal pre-existence of the Son of God, *as* Son of God! Not of an unknown divine person who *became* Son in manhood and through it, at the incarnation. We proclaim him Son with the Father in everlasting divine relationship or ever the world was, from eternity: without beginning of days, one who is Son by divine nature. The faith confesses three divine persons in the eternal relationship of Father, Son, and Holy Ghost, subsisting in one divine essence from everlasting to everlasting.

How can these erroneous people—particularly Taylor Brethren—profess three separate, unrelated divine persons in eternity, without avoiding the blasphemy of the worst of arch-heretics—three gods? How shall they rob God of his distinctive, divine, and eternal relationships in Father, Son, and Holy Ghost, without reducing those relations to temporal office, mere official function, a by-product of flesh and blood, bone and tissue, earth and time? How dare they do this? How dare they assert that all that makes the Father, Father—is office; the Son, Son—is function? And at that, merely from the Advent?

Yet droves of these heretics, scattered by the Almighty from their Taylor Brethren halls, now lurk entirely undetected in numerous Open Brethren, Christian Brethren, Baptist, Anglican, and other 'churches' and Halls. How *this* shows up the apostasy of our day. They simply don't care. Not about Christ.

Since the relationship is asserted to be inherently non-existent, the names actually figurative, the choice of which of the divine persons took what relative place merely arbitrary, then the Father might have been the Son, the Spirit could have been the Father, and the Son as easily the Spirit, but for that temporal and arbitrary choice of office! Horrible blasphemy. The very use of the intimate relationships predicated of the Eternal God, shows the essential mystery:—and despite all the evil reasoning of man, *mystery* it shall remain

—three distinct divine persons, yet so inexplicably, mysteriously and spiritually united in the eternal communion of Father, Son, and Holy Ghost as to have being in but one divine essence, to be but one God.

What unbelieving rationalism lies behind the error that attacks this revealed truth! What a reducing of divine relationships to human limitations, eternal verities to temporal bounds, spiritual absolutes to materialistic confines. But faith looks up and soars above the relationship of father to son as men know it, with its obvious corollary of the previous existence of a father before ever the conception of his offspring—of separate generations divided by half a lifetime—I say, faith soars above that reasoning which rationalises from earth to heaven, time to eternity, men to God, creature to Creator, and the material to the spiritual.

And if these rationalists are so sincere, let them be sincerely consistent! For rationally and strictly the same bounds applied by them to the Son from human sonship must be deduced and applied paternally. By nature and name, a father himself must be subject to the same limitations in *his* generation as later apply to his offspring. With all these inadequacies—if their scheme *were* correct!—one would suppose the divine choice of a more suitable arbitrary office!

As to the Holy Spirit, it does not bother them that having already confounded themselves by rationalising from the twofold human relationship to the threefold relations of Father, Son, and Holy Ghost, they now find no parallel for the heavenly divine person of the Holy Ghost in a scheme predetermined by the limitations of their earthly, human and rationalising strictures. Not that they are humbled—or shamed —enough to suppose in themselves any limitation inherent in their few pounds of grey matter, soon to decay and be eaten by worms. No, nothing is too high or holy for *their* minds to doubt their right of ascent; nothing too infinite and impregnable that they suppose it to be past the dissecting abilities of *their* intellects. But where were they when the earth was formed out of nothing? When did they soar up to penetrate the infinite blackness beyond the stars?

Faith sees the relationship of Father and Son in terms of God himself, in his being called The Eternal: no shorter duration! Faith views the rationalizing of those relations from what applies to man—separate and distinct beginnings in sequence of generation—with real horror and repugnance. Faith believes the mystery of God in Father, Son, and Holy Ghost presented to it by the Spirit and the truth with peaceful and believing equanimity.

Faith knows that whatever faint glimmer the human relation between father and son shows of the divine, neither the fusion of male and female seed from which children take point of origin at conception, nor the fact of a point in time before which a son does not exist—and after which he has being— have anything remotely or possibly to bring to bear on the divine relationship to make it clearer, no matter how rationalized. On the contrary the evil and unbelieving rationalism that tries to make it so, attempts with rude hands to pull eternity into time, the everlasting into beginnings, God down to men, and heaven to earth.

What parallel *can* exist between the father-son relation seen in terms of time and humanity—that!—and the eternal subsistence of three persons who are spirit, in one essence which is God, united in the spiritual and perpetual intimacy of a threefold union in eternal life which ever stood in the mystery of the divine relationships of Father, Son, and Holy Ghost?

Whatever the erroneous may say, however loudly they might trumpet their belief—*belief?*—in three unknown, unnamed and unrelated divine persons, however they may cry persecution on the grounds that they are misunderstood—they are not at all correct: they are all too well understood—the truth is that they are on sandy ground, they are in miry clay, they are taken in the snare, their foot has stumbled, and into the pit which they have digged for others they themselves have fallen.

Cut away all the textual padding, all the devotional platitudes, all the superfluous accuracies, what remains is that at heart they wish to rationalize the inexplicable and to intellectualize the mystery. It is unreasonable to them to accept the revelation of the eternal Son without a beginning. Yet they cannot assert that Christ's sonship had a commencement, without bringing on their heads the charge of denying his deity by questioning his eternity! What is left to them, but to take the relationship out of eternity into time and say 'he is Son from the incarnation only'; to take it out of deity into manhood and say 'sonship is descriptive of his humanity, not his divinity.' But they are altogether at fault. Heretically at fault.

And with what result? With this result: In this heresy the names Father, Son, and Holy Ghost can be nothing to do with God *in and of himself*; nothing to do with actual relationships of those divine persons in the Godhead; no, they are temporal situations caused by the creation of the manhood of Christ, which they call, Sonship. Dreadful! And since they say that what makes this unknown divine person *Son*, is the incarnation, then the Father was not Father before the incarnation but an unknown and—presumably—divine, person. Then how can they avoid the conclusion, an unknown god? The Spirit was not the Spirit before the incarnation but an unknown and—presumably—divine person. Again, how can they avoid the conclusion, an unknown god?

What is now discovered is that *without the eternal, living and spiritual relationships of Father, Son, and Holy Ghost it is impossible to avoid the inference of three unknown gods!* The very relationship—once seen as eternal, once conceived of as spiritual, once owned as living—implies an inconceivable oneness, an inseparable unity, a merging spirituality, an inter-flowing of eternal life, that whilst not *explaining* the mystery of three persons in One God, *makes it believable.* By robbing God of his names and nature, *these heretics make it unbelievable.*

The truth is, precisely because of the quickening being and vital intimacy in the very life-union of these divine inter-relationships, we who hold them *can* assert three divine persons, *because* the intimacy itself indicated in these relations, once translated in terms of the spiritual and eternal, proclaims but One God! The Son has his own distinct life yet it is from out of the ever-quickening life of the Father. The Spirit has his own separate being yet as flowing perpetually from the inner life of the Son: and this subsisting from eternity in God who is a spirit.

Thus whilst proclaiming three distinct divine persons, we perceive an inter-flowing, an inseparable merging, an under-lying subsistence, an eternal life, which, in its oneness, clearly proclaims the union of three persons in one divine essence, and one essence in three divine persons. Precisely because the relationship of Father, Son, and Holy Ghost is not of time and never began: exactly for the reason that the relationship is wholly and divinely spiritual, being nothing to do with anything that has been created and made: I say, precisely, exactly, therefore we see—albeit in a mystery—but one God in the unity of three distinct divine persons.

The designations of Father, Son, and Holy Ghost—used in revelation because they *are* what subsists in deity—are seen marvellously to proclaim the everlasting name and nature of God, by the coming of the Son. The One who took that lowly place in incarnation so as to reveal the Godhead in the Father, could not hide his own everlasting glory, any more than could be hid that of the eternal Spirit. It is by the hints of divine mysteries and by the glimpses of eternal relationships between the Father and the Son, that we perceive what was from everlasting, as it is by real spiritual experience that we are enabled to say of Father, Son, and Holy Ghost—as such and in that relationship—'from everlasting to everlasting thou art God!'

Therefore although the manifestation of God came in with the incarnation of the Son, the divine relationships certainly did not! Those relationships—unveiled in the coming of the Son—existed from eternity. And although the revelation of God is declared in the Father through the lowly place taken by the Son as man, and through the lowlier taken by the Holy Spirit sent to glorify Christ, yet that revelation is none the less one of the equal deity of three divine persons in one God. Equal, I say; for all that it was brought to light by the staggering condescension and awe-inspiring humility of the Son and of the Spirit.

Yet astonishingly, heretics will still deny this truth, and pressed, will fall back upon scriptures hard to be understood, which these unstable and unlearned persons wrest to their own destruction and to the confusion of the gullible. As though scripture supported the destructive notion that Christ's Sonship existed only in his manhood, as if it were neither in deity nor from eternity! One such instance of this wresting of scripture is seen in the decree of Psalm 2:7, so readily misapplied by these heretics, yet in fact teaching quite the opposite to what they suppose.

But consider this passage: 'I will declare the decree: the LORD hath said unto me, Thou art my Son; this day have I begotten thee.'

Boldly laying hold of the difficulty in interpreting the words 'begotten' and 'this day', the heretics who derogate the eternal sonship of Christ attempt to make out that the statement 'this day', limits the title 'Son' to that point in time when he was 'begotten'—that *day*—and hence refuse to entertain the truth of the relationship of Father and Son from *eternity*.

But how puerile! For observe that before the place in the verse where it is said 'this day have I begotten thee', and therefore before the point in time referred to as 'this day', I say, before both these things it had already been stated, 'the LORD hath said unto me, Thou *art* my Son.' Now, when was that said? In the past: '*hath* said'. In the past: that is, eternity past. And if in eternity past, then prior to the day present when as to incarnate manhood the ancient prophecy would be fulfilled 'this day have I begotten thee'. It is evident that both verse and decree refer to the pre-existent Son *as Son*, before going on to reveal the decree *concerning that same pre-existent Son*, as it pertains to his incarnation—or resurrection—one day in time.

Therefore 'this day have I begotten thee' refers to one who was the Son already: 'Thou Art'. It concerns one of whom the I AM of eternity perpetually says to the THOU ART of everlasting, in a way of ever-present continuity: *Thou art my Son*. This Sonship being of the divine ever-present—*art*—it cannot be affected by creation, time, incarnation, death, resurrection or ascension. It reflects that which is: namely, the state of relationship from eternity to eternity. This prophecy is recorded of the incarnation—or perhaps resurrection—of the eternal Son a thousand years before he came into the world. So the Father declares to the Son, by name, *then*—one thousand years before the event—the future of a thousand years to come, by these words *at that time*: Thou art—not, thou wilt be: thou *art*; one thousand years before the incarnation—thou *art* my Son.

This Psalm is quoted by the apostle Paul—Acts 13:33—during his discourse on the sabbath day in the synagogue at Antioch of Pisidia. In the address, Paul gives a brief history of Israel up to David the King; he speaks of John the Baptist's testimony to Christ; thence going on to declare the Lord's death and resurrection. Proceeding to testify that the Lord Jesus was risen indeed, Paul affirms that there were eye-witnesses: 'He was seen many days of them which came up with him from Galilee.'

Furthermore there were ancient records which foretold of that resurrection. First, the promise to the fathers fulfilled in the raising up of Jesus. Second, the prophecy in Psalm 2, 'as it is also written'—as well as the written promise of resurrection, *also* the written prophecy of it—'in the second psalm, Thou art my Son, this day have I begotten thee.' Without a doubt, the apostle is applying Psalm 2:7 not now to the preceding incarnation but to the subsequent resurrection of Jesus from the grave, and it is as bodily raised from the dead that he applies the passage to the Son as 'begotten this day'.

From which I conclude indubitably that it was not his divine sonship as such absolutely, separately, and distinctly, which was begotten that day—the day of the resurrection—but necessarily it was the Son as having united humanity to himself in manhood, that the Father thus begat from the dead on the day of resurrection. It was in terms of the then dead and buried body which the Son had assumed in incarnation when he took manhood into union with his divine person. 'He hath raised up Jesus again; as it is also written in the second psalm, Thou art my Son, this day have I begotten thee.' It was in his *humanity* that the Son rose again from the dead, on the day in which God raised him from the grave according to the ancient prophecy.

It is not right to over-simplify the complex nature of the person of Christ and loosely apply to his manhood what is proper to his deity, or to his divinity that which concerns his manhood, nor to either divinity or humanity those references that take in both natures in one person. If one is to speak of Christ *it must be with care, humbly within the scope of one's own spiritual perception*, and only *then* as called and led by the Spirit and in the fear of God.

Therefore it is abundantly evident that those who deny the eternal sonship of Christ have in fact compounded their error by their misinterpretation of Psalm 2:7. For if they themselves had taken their erroneous views of Sonship more seriously—that their error asserts unknown and unrelated divine persons taking the 'office' of Father and Son at the birth of Jesus Christ —then they would have seen that, for them, the resurrection could not be on 'this day', because, on the contrary, to them 'this day' would have to have been that of the incarnation. But beyond all dispute Paul applies it to the day of the resurrection, Acts 13:33. Will they then adjust and tell us that he was not Son between the incarnation and the resurrection? If so, why did he constantly during that period lift up his eyes to heaven, saying, 'Father'? If not, since Paul applies 'Thou art my Son' to the resurrection and not to the incarnation, what was he between the two? If they answer 'Son', then by the same token we reply, 'And as he was before the resurrection, so was he before the incarnation, that is, *eternally* Son.'

But what of the *inherited* name of Son declared by Hebrews 1:4-5, in the latter verse of which the second psalm is quoted? Since the idea of inheritance is that of the future possession of what at the time is promised only, superficially it appears that the quotation might seem to give some buttress to this tottering fabrication of false sonship. But consider:

'Being made so much better than the angels, as he hath by inheritance obtained a more excellent name than they. For unto which of the angels said he at any time, Thou art my Son, this day have I begotten thee?'

In the first verses of this chapter what is being emphasised is that God has spoken in his Son. Up to the coming of the Messiah, God had spoken in a variety of ways and at various times, but now his speech is in—not by—'Son'. Regarding the content of that speech itself, nothing is said as yet; only that it is uttered 'in these last days'. What is now being set forth in fact is the Speaker, not the speech.

59

This is followed by a declaration of the qualifications of that Speaker. His qualifications are perfect, as one would expect of the Son of God. The sevenfold perfection of the Son as Speaker is seen, firstly, in that he is heir of all things; secondly, in that it was by him that God made the worlds. Thirdly, in that he is the brightness of God's glory, and fourthly, the express image of his person. The fifth qualification for this office of divine Speaker is that the Son upholds all things by the word of his power; the sixth thing we see is that it was by himself alone that he purged the sins of the people of God. Finally, so wonderful a preamble is crowned with glory to fulfil this sevenfold perfection, namely, that at present, now, he is seated on the right hand of the Majesty on high.

This is the point at which our quotation—Hebrews 1:4-5— commences, with Christ seen in terms of these qualifications, that history, those accomplishments, and in the position envisaged at the conclusion of the third verse. What a tremendous passage!

It is with this in mind that verse four opens with the words 'being made'. That is, *thus* being made: as ascended and glorified out of that mortifying humiliation, and therefore in consequence of his wonderful work in death. And if in death, then in manhood. As seated in majestic repose—having been raised from the dead in manhood—he is thus made so much better than the angels. Therefore it follows, being made *as man* so much better than the angels. It must be so. After all, there could never be any question of comparison between his divinity and the angels. But since he and they are compared, it follows that the comparison stands between them and the Son *in his risen manhood, with his work in manhood not only accomplished, but vindicated in resurrection and glorified in ascension.*

The accent is upon the glorious Son who was made man purging our sins, and therefore upon his prior abasement, his degrading crucifixion, his having been buried in the grave, yet now his being exalted, glorified, and ascended to the right hand of God. The emphasis is upon his being wonderfully honoured *as man once dead*, but now so perfectly vindicated and made *in that manhood* so much better than the angels. A position, an inheritance, *whatever* his eternal glory, *never occupied before*.

Therefore 'being made' refers to his exaltation, after his having been made man. And indeed his becoming man teaches that the Son *was* before being made man, because it was *he* that was so made. But the 'being made' of verse 4 is not merely being made flesh, because it refers to what he was made not only after assuming humanity but after being crucified, after death and burial, consequent upon the resurrection and as a result of the ascension.

I repeat, it stresses what he was made after his having 'purged our sins', after becoming dead as man—who was in his divine nature and person—but not in his manhood—everlasting and eternal, even the eternal SON. I say, after the SON became that, namely *man*, to do this, which is *purge our sins in death*, he was made as to risen manhood *in the following exalted status*: better in power, authority, and position than all the angels.

'So much better than the angels.' This is a comparison between the lofty elevation of the angels whom death does not affect, and the ascended glory of the Son who rose out of death. It demonstrates to what heights God raised his Son. The one who as man was humiliated in the world, and on earth died ignominiously, was buried and descended into the lower parts of the earth: this is he, who, as man, is now exalted so much higher than the angels. All this gives us the tone of the passage, and the sense of the context, summarising the cumulative doctrine leading the perceptive reader to appreciate the force of what follows. Now comes the passage in question.

'As he hath by inheritance obtained a more excellent name than they.' It does not surprise us that the advocates of this heretical error conclude that since the name of SON is said to be inherited, therefore it is not *inherent*. But that is to detach a sentence from the context simply because, isolated, it may then be forced to appear to tend towards their preconceived theory!

Their damnable theory. A theory to support which they desperately scan scripture to wrest out fragmentary statements and wrench away half-texts to heap up and garnish their little pile of 'proof'! The point is not what do they think, or I think, or other brethren think, or what did the reformers think, or what does anybody think, much less what does one *want* to think and therefore find in the passage, but, what is the mind of the Spirit? What is the genuinely unaffected drift of the passage in its context?

Doubtless in the first chapter of Hebrews the writer's purpose is to show by demonstration the superiority of the Son and of the Son's position. His pre-existent glory, his having been made flesh, his dying for sins, his rising, and finally his having ascended so high. And this *as man*, as ascended *man* over the angels. At this precise place in verse four, now the writer establishes his doctrine in terms of comparative *names*: '*as*'—as well as the height of his ascension over angels—'as he hath by inheritance obtained a more excellent name than they.' Hardly the time to show the supposed *limitation* of the name Son.

I reiterate, it is a comparative chapter. Where then is the comparison? Between what? Well, between angelic beings and the person of Jesus known as man below. But this same Jesus is actually the pre-existent eternal Son made man by assuming humanity into union with himself at the incarnation. Therefore notwithstanding this wonderful stoop of grace, all that is true of his divine nature is true of that person thus seen exalted. This is the reason why the first chapter of Hebrews opens by revealing that divinity which is his by nature as Son, before ever he was exalted in his nature as man on high after purging sins below!

The chapter reveals that the deity of the Son is unchanged and unaffected by that human nature taken into union with it, and unaffected even by his mortifying humiliation as man, so much so that his incarnation and death are assumed but not *actually stated* in the first four verses. His eternal sonship enhances, enriches and qualifies his manhood, thus making it effectual to do what the Son did by it: 'by himself purged our sins.'

Hence it is a question of the comparative difference between those named angels and he who is named Son. There *is* no comparison! Why make it? Because the first covenant was mediated by angels, and the second by the Son of God. The relative worth of the covenants is seen in the comparative quality of those to whom those covenants were entrusted respectively.

Comparison? But not solely between angels and the distinct *manhood* of Christ, but the whole *person* of Christ! Between angels and the Son then? Yes! Agreed it is the Son ascended as man: but the point is that the man in the place of death and burial was not *then* named Son in the emphasis upon his work: he was then named *Son of man* in the emphasis upon his work. He who was from everlasting the uncreated Son, who in point of time took human nature into union with himself in one person, then took that manhood into death as Son of man, just as now he takes it up in risen life as Son of God before the Majesty on high. Thus ascended, he is declared to be what he ever was in the mystery of his person: the Son! But now the Son seen in a unique newness, in a unique place, as beginning the new creation of glorified man. Thus he is seen as much above the angels, as his name from eternity was so utterly superior, so *inherently* better than theirs.

His divine name—though for a season obscured by humiliation, concealed in death, hidden through burial—is now openly declared in the inheritance of his risen Manhood to be what it ever was: *so much* better than the angels. Then what a difference in name between the Son and angels! The name angel is not an inherited name, neither is it an inherent one, nor was it a perpetual name: it is a created name. A given name to created spirits.

Not so the eternal Son. Certainly he may be viewed solely in terms of his created humanity. Equally he may be considered singularly in his divine nature everlastingly one with the Father and with the Holy Ghost. Again, the mystery of his person may be seen in the union of both natures in one without confusion or duality. It is in this latter sense, in the full mystery of that incarnate person, that he is set forth in these verses in Hebrews.

This Man who was born, lived, died, rose, ascended, and was thus made glorious, is yet in a mystery of union the person who was always and everlastingly the divine Son. It is his name—who is seen as ascended man—by right, and that not by creation, but of self-existent being: the Son. But now the eternal name is revealed as the everlasting inheritance of that glorified manhood.

The difficulty in understanding this verse arises solely from considering 'inheritance' with its *human limitations*, as something that comes to a man at a specific point in time, namely, after the death of the father. It is patently ridiculous and wholly impossible to think of transferring such a case to the circumstances of the Son. But if not, then the whole idea of inheritance must be profoundly qualified and treated in a manner unique to the manhood of the Son of God.

And of course the word inheritance—κληρονομία—will bear precisely the profound qualification and unique stress which the name of Son requires of it, in the sense that I have shown to be necessary. For it means *'what is obtained by lot'*, or *'what is obtained by possession'*. Not by *'death'* necessarily, observe. Now, what is the *possession* of the Eternal? When falls the *lot* of the Everlasting? Whatever, whenever, it is that, by *possession*, which the risen Son is said to have inherited.

The central difficulty in Heb. 1:4 lies in the fact that the Son is said to have inherited the name which he is elsewhere stated to have had from eternity: 'Being made so much better than the angels, as he hath by inheritance obtained a more excellent name than they.' But how can he inherit that name by which he has always been called? There is no doubt of the difficulty of this verse. Equally there is no doubt that the heretics deceitfully exploit that difficulty. But whatever the difficulty, and however they exploit it, and even if we could neither explain nor resolve it, *nothing alters the fact that scripture cannot, and does not, contradict itself*. Our obtuseness and ignorance concerning this verse *cannot alter what is taught elsewhere*. Neither can the verse contradict it. Then let not the heretics think to have gained so much as an inch to advance their heresy, even were we unable to resolve the apparent anomaly of this one passage.

And does the Son by inheritance obtain that more excellent name? Yes, he does. But he does not, for he cannot, *inherit* the name of Son *in the sense of his eternal Sonship, as to his divinity*. That name ever was, and ever shall be, his inherently. But he can, and he does, inherit the name of Son *in an entirely new, revealed, sense, as to his humanity*.

The Son, having become incarnate, in that humanity which he had taken into union with himself—a thing entirely new, entirely *added*, to his divine nature and being as Son— nevertheless took that manhood down into death. He really died. That man was dead and buried. For three days his dead body lay in the grave. But that is the *Son's* manhood! If so, what is become of the name of Son?

God raised him from the dead, and, risen and ascended, he who by himself purged our sins, is set down—*in the manhood that was lately dead and buried, the manhood, that is, of the Son*—set down at the right hand of the Majesty on high, for all that apparently unalterable, and final, humiliation of death. And what appears? Why, that, *for all the terrible humiliation*, this same Jesus was and is the eternal Son! 'Now, that he ascended, what is it but that he also descended first into the lower parts of the earth? *He that descended* is the same also that ascended up far above all heavens, that he might fill all things.' Before he descended, the name Son indicated in God, who is a spirit, divine relations in one divine essence, namely, Father, Son, and Holy Ghost, from everlasting. When he descended, he emptied himself; he laid aside his glory; nevertheless, though now seen in lowly manhood, yet here was the eternal Son. But who should declare his generation?

His manhood in his humiliation veiled it. His death in his crucifixion hid it. His burial seemed to contradict it. The grave and hell, the adversary and the powers of darkness, mocked it, as if to say, Where is the name of Son now? 'If thou be the Son of God, save thyself.' But he did not. He was crucified, dead, and buried, this Son of God, who was made of the seed of David according to the flesh. But after three days he rose again, he ascended on high, he sat down. Now, *there* is the name of the Son!

And where now is the mockery of the adversary? For, seated on the throne of glory, far above all heavens, *there* is seen the lot, *there* appears the inheritance of the Son in manhood. But, as with all inheritance, *it is assumed after death.* A death which for three days in the grave apparently eclipsed the name of Son. No more. The Son is risen indeed, and is set down in his Father's throne. But as never before. In a way unique. In a manner never seen from everlasting. In a word, *In risen Manhood.* Then, *as glorified Man, the Son comes into his everlasting inheritance.* 'As he hath by inheritance obtained a more excellent name.'

Yet the heretics now mock, as the devils then mocked, 'But if he be the eternal Son, how can he obtain the inheritance of his own name?' He obtained an inheritance just as an inheritance is always obtained: by death. But, uniquely, this was *his own* death. 'But if he were the eternal Son, How could he die?' In *manhood*. That is the key. He laid aside the glory of that name, to take the lowly place and name of Jesus, the Son of man. He was rejected. He was humiliated. He was crucified. Was this the *Son*? 'If thou be the Son of God, come down from the cross, and we will believe.' But he did not come down from the cross, and they did not believe, any more than the heretics now believe. Rather, he went down into the grave. His body was *buried out of sight*. He seemed to have lost all.

But he rose above all, that he might overcome all, and fill all. And when he rose, in himself he carried with him all those for whom he died, all those whose sins he had purged. He carried them in himself to glory. Now, *there* is an inheritance, and in the name of Son, for *that* is the name which from henceforth he shares with them. Ascended, after death, yet in manhood risen from the dead, he takes an entirely new position, both for himself and for his own. And in that new position, his full glory, laid aside as to deity at the incarnation, is taken up in glory at the ascension: the glory of the Son. That is what his manhood, and new manhood for multitudes, shows forth: the inheritance out of death of the name of Son.

Hebrews 2:4 is not therefore a comparison between the name of angels and the name of Son *in his absolute deity*. It is a comparison between the name of angels and the name of Son *in glorified manhood*. Then, a comparison between bringing in the old testament and the new testament respectively. If so, then a comparison between the angels having brought in the law, and the Son, his work on earth completed, ascended in glorious manhood, *there by right of inheritance to resume the glory he had once laid aside*, thus bringing in the gospel.

This resumption of his divine name, in terms of his humanity, is called 'Inheritance'. It does not for one moment call into question his eternal Sonship. Rather for eternity to come it glorifies his manhood with that Sonship. And not now in himself alone, but with him that great company which no man can number, whom he had redeemed by himself in death. All these riches, riches of grace, riches of glory, riches of Sonship, could only come by way of death: hence, no word is more suitable to set forth this truth than that which is used in this selfsame place, namely, 'Inheritance'.

But such is the obstinacy of these Plymouth 'Christian' Brethren of Taylor's—who now hide their name—that they still persist, 'If he is the eternal Son, how can he inherit the name of Son?' You see that they will not listen. Yet, since they are the blind followers of the blind, one would think that their other senses might be more acute. Not at all. Their deafness is as bad as their blindness: 'They are like the deaf adder, which stoppeth her ear; which will not listen to the voice of charmers, charming never so wisely.' And this is so of the followers of all heretics, that is, of all whom Satan has caught in his snare. Nevertheless we will take up our parable, and will not tire: 'If he is the eternal Son', they reiterate, 'How can he inherit the name of Son?'

Because the inheritance is not to him in *that* form—'the form of God'—nor in his name *as indicative of what subsisted in deity from eternity*. How can this be? Because he is not said to have inherited it in his deity, which is absolutely impossible. He is said to have inherited it in his humanity, which is altogether suitable.

The inheritance is *after the glory of the form of God was laid aside*, and another form, that of crushing humiliation in manhood, assumed. 'Being in the form of God, he thought it not robbery to be equal with God: but made himself of no reputation, and took upon him the form of a servant, and was made in the likeness of men: and being found in fashion as a man, he humbled himself, and became obedient unto death, even the death of the cross.' From thence, the inheritance.

Having finished his work in manhood, that is, having died for his people, the smitten, stricken, and afflicted man of humiliation, he *then* showed just who it was that had taken that form, and submitted to such a death, even the death of the cross. Then, I say, he showed just who he was, just how glorious he is, and just what unapproachable light in deity is proper to him. But he showed this *in the same manhood as that in which he had been humiliated, and in which through death he had redeemed his people.* And thus that manhood is said to 'inherit' in the ascension, for himself and for his people, the name of Son, once as to its glory laid aside in humiliation. But now in the fulness of that glory, radiant in the inheritance, for himself and his people—for he brought many sons to glory—there appears the fulness and consummation of the Father's good pleasure in the Son: 'This is my beloved Son, in whom I am well pleased.'

Now therefore he who would limit the eternal sonship of Christ must of necessity dismiss the Son's inheritance, sever eternal relationships, deny perpetual Fatherhood, limit unending eternity, annihilate everlasting constancy, dissolve absolute immutability; he must plunder heaven, he must raze the sanctuary, he must trample divinity, he must thrust his nihilistic hand into the very reaches of infinity, he must intrude his anarchistic mind into the immutable counsels of the Godhead: *but these things cannot be done!* He who attempts them shall be snared and taken, the rock shall fall on him, and, at the last, he shall be ground to powder.

III

By the Operation of the Spirit

'The angel answered and said unto Mary, The
Holy Ghost shall come upon thee.'

Luke 1:35

THIS is the first statement in answer to Mary's question
'*How shall this*'—conception—'*be, seeing I know not a man?*'
It is a declaration that takes precedence over the reference to
the oversight of the Father—'*the power of the Highest shall overshadow thee*'—and over the incarnation of the Son—'*shall be
called the Son of God*'—because it alludes to that which makes
the advent a reality. It refers to the immediate creative work
actually to take place upon Mary so as to effect the framing
and formation of the promised seed in the womb of the virgin.

This is the work of the Holy Ghost, and it differs from the
authoritative direction, divine purpose, and heavenly oversight of the Highest at the incarnation. The Father directed
the work, oversaw that event, and determined its execution
in point of time, act of divinity, detail of providence, and form
of creation. However, the work of the Father is distinct from
that of the Son whom he sent, just as it is separate from that
of the Holy Ghost whom he directed.

Furthermore the work of the Spirit indicated by '*The Holy
Ghost shall come upon thee*', is in fact another thing than the

act of the Son of God in assuming humanity and being made flesh. The work of the Holy Ghost in coming upon Mary so as to form from her seed that in which the Son would become incarnate is a work that is unique. It is the creative act peculiar to and distinctive of the person of the Holy Ghost, according to the will of God and the Father.

Withal, perfect harmony is seen in the blending together of the work of the Spirit upon Mary, together with that of the Son as uniting to himself what was thus formed from her, the whole being under the omniscient direction of God and the Father overshadowing Mary from on high. What a wonderful display of divine activity is seen in Father, Son, and Holy Ghost as brought to light by the advent of Christ! God in three persons is revealed through the divinely essential contribution in grace made by each, the sum of which is the very expression of the unity of the Godhead, thus manifest by the coming into the world of the Son of God to effect salvation and bring in the divine purpose.

Thus—if we are to understand the doctrine—on the one hand we must apprehend the perfect harmony of the simultaneous work of God as such in the incarnation, and on the other hand we must distinguish between 'The Holy Ghost ... The Highest ... and the Son of God', Luke 1:35. Conversely in giving attention to the singular contribution of one distinct divine person, it is then that we must not forget for a moment the flowing together in unity, at one and the same time, of the threefold exercise of God in the one great work that brought about the coming of the Son into the world.

Whence it follows that in focusing upon the creative work of the Holy Ghost—'the Holy Ghost shall come upon thee'—we must remember the instantaneous oversight of the Father at and upon every stage of this work. Likewise we must not lose sight of the simultaneous response of the Son—equally under the direction of the Father—answering to that work of the

Spirit, in uniting to himself the humanity and taking upon him the body prepared at the moment of its creation.

It is in this sense and this sense alone, that 'the Word was made flesh', John 1:14. Not that—under the direction of the Father—the Son himself made that flesh, much less made himself into it; the very distinction itself observed in the divine activity becomes the safeguard which prevents one from falling into error. The mere fact of the work of the Spirit in the incarnation shows that there was that prepared of the Holy Ghost which the Son was to take into union with himself.

Let there be no mistake: the observation of this distinction in the activity of divine persons matters enormously. It teaches us that the Holy Ghost acted as creator to prepare wholly the substance and life which the eternal Son took into union with himself: that it was ready, as such, for his advent: that it was prepared by creation for his incarnation. This in itself instructs us that Christ did not prepare, form, frame, or create that humanity by his coming: the Holy Ghost had prepared, formed, framed and created it for the coming of the Son of God.

Therefore it follows that there was no change in the nature of the Son's deity when he was made flesh: the Godhead of Christ was not changed, but the Word was made flesh in flesh prepared of the Holy Ghost under the direction of the Father. The Word was made flesh not changed into it. The Son took flesh into union, he was not converted into it; the prepared flesh was there for him to take and he took it in the incarnation. Hence I say, his deity was not converted to humanity, but, as the Word, was manifest through that behind which it was veiled. Union is not conversion! Converting one nature into another is not uniting two distinct natures! But in the incarnation the Son of God united two distinct natures in his one person.

What I am saying is that the fact of the Holy Spirit having created the human nature and frame from Mary's seed for the Son's coming, shows in itself that the Son united what was prepared for him unto himself. This fact alone refutes the error that in coming he changed himself into something that he had not been. Changing one nature into another is transubstantiation, not incarnation.

What occurred in incarnation was that the divine person of the eternal Son, everlastingly possessed of divine nature, united with that nature in his own person the human nature and body prepared by the Holy Ghost from the virgin Mary; this he did in the instant of its creation under the direction of the Father, so as to possess in the integrity of his own being the mystery of two distinct natures in the integrity of his one person.

Nevertheless in safeguarding the truth that the incarnation of the everlasting Son of God involved neither change nor alteration to his divine nature, equal care is required to avoid opposite extremes as regards his human nature. That is, one end of the spectrum of error may impugn his deity by supposing that it was reduced in and by the incarnation, but the other extremity will confuse his humanity by inferring that it was not human nature which the Son took into union, but that it was a human *person* whom the Son united to himself in the incarnation.

But the advent was not a union of two *persons*. The Son of God did not indwell a human person of unique origin called Jesus. On the contrary, the name Jesus was given to the Son of God to signify his becoming incarnate in the body prepared and uniting to his divinity the human nature created. Therefore, far from the incarnation being a union of two persons, one divine and one human, it was a union of two *natures* in *one person*. The Son of God—ever possessed of divine nature— was from the advent manifest through the flesh in which he was made, and expressed in the human nature which he took into union with the divine at the incarnation.

All this shows how vitally important it is to see distinctly what was the work of the Holy Ghost at the conception and birth of Jesus Christ. What, precisely, did the Spirit himself alone effect? Exactly what was it in and of itself that the Spirit of God brought in, as a result of his operation for and at the coming of the Son of God into the world? What did the Holy Ghost create at the incarnation? These are the questions that faith will and must ask, as seeking to exalt the Lord Jesus Christ aright. And these are the questions before which ignorance must quail and error shrink, being unable to stand the responsive light required by such penetrating enquiry as this which magnifies the work of God in Christ.

Thus, how many errors are slain at birth by a right view of incarnation! By the slinging of this one small smooth stone and that right early, Goliath falls mortally wounded at the outset, whilst as yet four stones still remain untouched in the scrip of sound doctrine. The apostle Paul directs our minds to this fact when immediately following the trumpet-blast with which he commences the epistle to the Romans—'the gospel of God concerning his Son Jesus Christ our Lord'—he adds the clarion call: 'Which was made of the seed of David according to the flesh', Romans 1:3. By this early presentation of the Ark of the Testimony of God, the idols of error fall immediately; only the stump of Dagon is left to him: he is fallen; his hands are cut off at the threshold.

Observe that the apostolic gospel declares that it is the Son who was already in being who was then afterwards made of the seed of David according to the flesh. This absolutely requires the Son's prior existence in order that he should be thus made. And since before becoming flesh he appears under the name Son, I deduce from this that not only was the Son pre-existent, but that he was so in the name and relationship *of* Son. Moreover that this relationship was divine because it was with the Father, God withal. Furthermore the doctrine that 'he was made' precludes his making himself or changing

74

his nature: on the contrary it argues the body prepared, and if so, prepared by the Holy Ghost under the power of the Highest.

Finally, since the seed of David in promise is the seed of the woman by prophecy, then that which *was* made, was made from woman alone, and therefore had all the properties of human nature but none of the essential quality of a separate human person. In any event that seed never had separate existence of itself, for immediately, as Mary conceived of the Holy Ghost, so the Son of God took that humanity into union with himself and became incarnate.

The selfsame teaching is to be found in Galatians 4:4, 'God sent forth his Son, made of a woman, made under the law.' As soon as this seed was created by the Holy Ghost, then it was that the pre-existent Son of God—he *was* the Son, evidently, before God sent him forth—took that created humanity into union with himself in the womb of the virgin by incarnation. It is in this sense, I say, that the Son was 'made of the seed of David according to the flesh.' Once this is seen in its true light scales fall from the eyes: it is then of necessity that error, vanquished, quits the field.

How carefully the writers of holy writ observed these refined and spiritual distinctions: and no wonder, for these holy men were moved and breathed upon within by the Holy Ghost. The epistle to the Hebrews in the first chapter maintains this same doctrine, declaring the divinity of the Son with these words: 'Thou, Lord, in the beginning hast laid the foundation of the earth.' His pre-existence as such is asserted in a subsequent verse of the next chapter: 'Forasmuch then as the children are partakers of flesh and blood, he also himself likewise took part of the same.'

In that latter verse, notice the two partakers: 'the children' and 'he also himself'. These are the *persons* involved, first, the human persons of the elect children of God, and then the divine person of the eternal Son of God. But next observe the nature of the one thing partaken in common by both: 'flesh and blood', called in the case of the person of the Son, 'the same'. Flesh and blood does not indicate a person, but a *nature*; neither solely body, for the word *flesh* has a far wider meaning in scripture than the mere substance. The persons of the children partook the body and nature indicated by 'flesh and blood', being human persons expressed in human nature. The *person* of the Son likewise *partook the same*—stupendous miracle!—the same *nature*, uniting that which the Holy Ghost had created with his divine nature in *one person*.

From this it is clearly seen that the doctrine—regarding the humanity of Christ which was formed by the Holy Ghost in the womb of the virgin—hinges upon the vital distinction between *nature* and *person*. It may be objected, has been objected, that this is a distinction without a difference. Not at all. Such an objection reveals no lack of difference in the distinction, but a great deal of indifference—to blasphemy as well as ignorance—on the part of the persons objecting.

The word Nature is derived from the Latin *natura* birth, course of things; this in turn coming from *nasci* to be born. It is defined as: 'The essential qualities of a thing; the inherent and inseparable *combination of properties*'—my italics—'essentially pertaining to anything and giving its fundamental character.' (Shorter Oxford English Dictionary).

We can hardly think of such a definition of nature as separate in human beings from person. Indeed, in every case of mankind save one, human nature is coetaneous with person. Invariably, in the human race nature is inseparable from person: it cannot subsist of itself, it is in and from birth 'the general and inherent character or disposition of mankind', it is the 'inherent power or force by which the physical and mental activities of men are sustained'.

76

Human nature gives mankind its fundamental character as humanity, and it is that through which man expresses his personality. Yet to be strictly accurate, since *men* have that fundamental character, and *they* express their personality *through* that human nature, in humanity itself there is a genuine and precise difference between person and nature, albeit the one cannot exist without the other in reality, and the distinction is not often made in practice.

But when one considers the person of Christ, and his unique manhood, it is quite another matter. Here no looseness can be tolerated. In the singular case of the unique Man we must, to declare that manhood, really emphasise his *truly human nature*. Notwithstanding, to avoid the grotesque aberration of Duality—the revolting error that the divine person of the Son indwelt the human *person* of Jesus, making Christ two persons, one divine and one human—I say, to avoid the heresy of Duality, we must strenuously assert that the human nature created by the Holy Ghost from the seed of the woman *was not a distinct person*, but was in fact that unique human nature taken into union by the divine person of the Son of God. Thus, the distinction is not only valid but absolutely essential.

Very well, but what constitutes human nature? What are its essential qualities? If it is a 'combination of properties' giving to a person his fundamental character as a human being, then what are those properties, short of the person to whom they belong?

Although one generally thinks of human nature in terms of the intangible soul as opposed to the tangible body, strictly the body itself must be included as an essential part of human nature. The body is indisputably one of the essential properties giving to humanity its fundamental character as mankind; men cannot exist as human beings without that human frame. Thus in the strictest sense one must state that human nature consists of two media, one tangible and material and the other intangible and immaterial.

Therefore I say that the tangible medium of human nature consists of the human body in the sum of its parts interior and exterior, constituted by the wonderful organism and cellular structure of so many different refined and delicate systems combining in one to give physical expression to the term Human Being, and in the case of each singular person under that heading to give a distinct and personal manifestation to that wonderful physical nature. It is such a nature, unique, spotless and impeccable, that was created by the Holy Ghost from the seed of the woman for the incarnation of the Son of God: 'A body hast thou prepared me'.

Notwithstanding, it is generally the second medium, that of the immaterial and intangible, to which one refers when speaking of human nature. This in itself falls into two parts. The first part being constituted by the essential properties of the soul in which the person gives expression to himself, and the second being the actual life of that soul.

I do not deny for one moment that the intangible properties of the soul are most intimately related to the physical counterparts with which they correspond. For instance, the highly complicated cellular structure of the brain, the delicate organisms of the nervous system, the intrinsically vital biochemical elements and substances: all these are essential to the processes of physical life, the characteristics of nature, the mental apparatus, and with the functions of the sensibility. As to life itself, the intimacy of the bond between the physical and the abstract is amazingly revealed from the very beginning by these words: 'The life is in the blood.'

However it is in the blending of life with the intangible properties of the soul that the closest interrelation of these things is seen, in the wonderful harmony of the fusion together into one of all the parts of human nature. Here also is traced the work of the Holy Ghost in creating humanity for the assumption of the Son of God: life of Mary's life was in the seed, and from it the Holy Ghost gave true human vitality to all the essential properties of that humanity, to the human nature of the Lord Jesus.

Having noted that the body is really a part of total human nature, in the general use of the term I have observed that the emphasis is usually placed upon the two intangible factors of that whole sum, namely upon the life itself, and more especially upon the fundamental properties of the soul.

I have sought to make equally plain that the life is very close to the person proper, but strictly, the *person* lives, the life does not live itself. The intangible qualities of human nature are also most intimately related to the life itself, as also to the physical means of expression and beyond all these to the actual person expressed. Yet notwithstanding, the whole of the nature—whether life, body or soul—is distinct from the essential self-conscious person himself. All that is definite and clear.

Now I proceed to elucidate what is meant by 'The essential properties of the soul'. I repeat, human nature includes the body, as it also involves the life. However it has been affirmed that human nature incorporates those combined properties of the immaterial soul by which—above all—expression to humanity is given. What are these properties? That is the question.

The essential properties of the soul are threefold: they are mental, emotional and volitional. The mental faculties may be regarded as exterior and interior. The exterior mental faculties consist first of all, in the intelligence—Latin *inter* between, and *legere* to bring. This is referred to in the Greek of the new testament as the 'sunesis'—*σύν* with, *ἵημι* to send. The intelligence is that part of the mental processes which functions as the confluence of the five senses, to which data from them flows, and by which it is identified.

79

This process of identification is in connection with the second exterior mental faculty, namely, the memory—Latin *memoria*, 'the faculty by which things are remembered'; Greek μνήμη . Thus data, having been received, is now identified; from thence it is absorbed and finally processed by the third, deeper, mental faculty. The function of the first two faculties—intelligence and memory—now appears to be that to and from which intelligence of what is perceived by the senses flows variously, being then collated and recorded, after which process of judgment is given.

The third, and deeper, exterior mental faculty is the intellect proper—perhaps the Latin *intellectus*—called in the new testament the φρόνημα , where undoubtedly the reference is to the thinking processes themselves as they respect identified data passed from the intelligence. This is the faculty which subjects to the thought process all the external data passed to it via the intelligence from the exterior world. Hence strictly this is the constitutional faculty created to answer to *phenomena* —what is real, apparent, sensible, and therefore of external and worldly intelligence—only and as such.

So much for the exterior mental faculties. The interior mental faculties on the other hand are concerned properly with data from another and deeply internal source, namely the consciousness. The consciousness is that in which is inherent the intuitive knowledge of those first truths and religious verities so important to the soul. I say, it is in the consciousness that these things are revealed, in the interior mind, and no external worldly data of any description can be compared remotely with the vast importance of such inherent first truths as, for example, the Deity; law; right and wrong; moral obligation; worship; humanity; sin; life; death; judgment; resurrection; immortality; eternity: and suchlike solemn realities. The faculty created to be occupied constitutionally with such profound and monumental matters is the rational faculty, the reason—Latin *reri* to think—called in the Greek λόγος, in this sense, 'reason as a faculty, creative reason'.

This faculty of the inner mind is that in the use of which the mentality finds true coherence, and without which the mental condition is unconstitutional and actually chaotic. It is the faculty in man answering to the *rationale*, or Λόγος of the universe, and is concerned not at all with *phenomena*, material evidence, but finds its better part as wholly occupied with the more elevated truths illuminated by the *noumena* in the intuitive consciousness.

Now passing on from the mentality, the next essential property of the soul is the sensibility. The sensibility consists of the emotional faculties which again may be regarded as interior and exterior. The exterior faculties correspond with the physical appetites, as they do also with the mental cravings, answering emotively to the external senses. They consist of the affections and desires 'of the flesh and of the mind', and involve a considerable range of constitutional and involuntary propensities.

As to the interior emotional faculties, it is a question of the deeper sensibility as related to the will itself. Where the will is involved the corresponding state of feeling is profound and may be extremely powerful, and it is here that the passions, proper, are discovered. Other interior emotional faculties, perhaps more related to the interior mental processes, are the imagination in which the fantasy plays a distinct part, and the conscience, decisively emotional in its function of sensibly monitoring the response of the will to the conscious awareness of right and wrong in the mentality.

The will is the third and last essential property of the soul, and is most profoundly at the seat of human nature. There are some three classes of voluntary action in the activity of the will, the first of which may be defined as the immediate intention. It is by this that the physical and mental processes were created to be controlled rationally and according to the light of inner consciousness, and in connection with which the range of exterior emotions were formed to register with feeling.

Of course one speaks objectively, considering the will—as in the case of the other essential properties of the soul—first and foremost from the viewpoint of what this was *created to be*, not what in fact subjectively *it became*—alas—in the Fall, and in consequence of the disordering havoc of inbred sin. I speak methodically, of human nature in itself as it ought to have been, not in that degeneration which it has become in fact. I am dealing with human nature objectively in and of itself. This method in any event and in all circumstances being the only possible basis and premise upon and with which to begin any understanding of the nature of mankind.

The second class of the voluntary action of the will I refer to as the proximate resolution, being concerned with the choice of ways and means to the end for which the soul lives and moves and has its being. That end of being, as regards volition, is the subject of the third and final voluntary action: that which I call the ultimate purpose.

This ultimate purpose is the fixed resolution on which the 'heart' is set, governing the whole being, directing all the faculties, purposing all the life force: it is the 'single eye' causing 'the whole body' to be full either of 'light' or of 'darkness'. It is the 'good' or 'bad' tree resolving the nature of all the fruit ever to grow thereon; it is the 'heart' which lives for the soul's treasure, and where that treasure is, there will the heart be also, for this heart 'cannot serve two masters'.

Now I assert that each and all of the features heretofore described are what is meant by *human nature*, and that *the man* Christ Jesus was possessed of each feature and the sum of them all. That is to say, the perfect humanity of Jesus Christ entailed a real and true body possessed not only of bones, sinews, flesh and blood but also of brain, nervous system, and vital energy. With this body Jesus possessed true human life. Further to that living frame Christ Jesus had all the essential properties of the soul: the intangible mental faculties were expressed by his human life through that tangible brain; the immaterial sensibility was manifest in his humanity diffusing the material and feeling nervous system; and the abstract volition was active in his physical life force and vital energy proper to him as man.

This is demonstrated by numerous texts and passages in the gospels. As has been said, Jesus was volitional and willed, he was sensitive and felt, he was rational and given to thought. His was true humanity, his was a real human nature, in his perfection he possessed the genuine life of mankind, and his impeccable body expressed true manhood. *This* is what the operation of the Holy Ghost created from the seed of the woman, and did so for the immediate incarnation of the person of the Son of God, and for the concurrent assumption of that created human nature into union with his everlasting divine nature.

But notwithstanding that his human nature was so perfect, withal that his humanity was so fearfully and wonderfully made—'marvellous are thy works, and that my soul knoweth right well'—withal that in the Father's book all his members were written and his substance yet being unformed was not hid from the overshadowing of the Most High; I say, withal that God possessed his reins and covered him in his mother's womb—'How precious are thy thoughts to him, O God! how great is the sum of them'—still for all this wonderful and complex truth his human nature was *not* a separate human person: *it was human nature* and human nature alone.

Having arrived at this point, the question that presses upon the mind is this: then what lacks the human nature of Christ, that a human *person* possesses? If so much be his as possessed of human nature, what is not his that makes the vital distinction in humanity between nature and person? In fine, subtract *nature* from *person*: what is left?

In answering this enquiry the correct procedure—first and foremost—is to compare the conception of Jesus Christ with that of every other single human being save Adam. Immediately the difference leaps to the attention of the enquirer. Persons come into being in the womb of the mother at conception, with the penetration of the female seed by that of the male. The consequent entity is no longer simply the seed of the woman, nor yet only that of the man, but it is the result of the fusion into one of the two seeds in a new, separate, distinct being not in existence before.

The indispensable conditions for the coming into being of human persons are, properly: man, woman, physical union, and—in consequence—the fertile penetration of the female seed by the male, resulting in a distinct and separate living entity fused from the two into one at conception, thence to be nurtured in the womb until birth. It is this entity that is called a person.

But in the coming into the world of Jesus Christ certain of these indispensable conditions did not exist. Moreover *that* kind of conception never took place. So we are dealing with what is unique, and that because it is divinely miraculous. We are handling what is ultimately inexplicable, and this because it is a supernatural mystery. Nevertheless in what is miraculous and mystical what is to be *believed* by the faithful should be most carefully taught.

Hence I enquire: What are the indispensable conditions for the existence of human persons that did not obtain in the birth of Jesus Christ? What is always true of human conception, that was not true of his conception? The answer is both obvious and clear: In the case of Jesus Christ there was—as to his manhood—no father, no physical union, no male seed, no penetration of the female seed, and therefore no resultant union from the fusion of male and female seed into one. Hence there could be no human entity called a person.

Then what in the case of Jesus Christ was in common with the normal and regular conception and birth of mankind? A woman, a true mother. Her seed, the real and physical seed of the woman. *But nothing else whatever.* How then could conception take place? I answer, it could and did take place because the Holy Ghost came upon her, and because the power of the Highest overshadowed her: therefore also that holy thing that was born of her—of *her*, from *her* seed—was called the Son of God. Thus in a mystery was conceived the genuine reality of true human nature. But the *person* to whom that human nature belonged and belongs, was and is the eternal Son of God. That is the superlative divinity and staggering miracle of the incarnation.

The existence of a person results from that original quickening into being as a distinct entity, of the fused male and female seeds at conception. This is always accompanied by and expressed through the physical and moral nature. But that natural quickening into one person of the two seeds, male and female, never happened in the case of Jesus Christ. His human nature was created directly by the Holy Ghost from the seed of the woman alone: it is *that* which the Holy Ghost effected in his operation. Therefore his humanity is at once unique and miraculous in its origin, as it is singular and peerless in its design.

That is why we can and *must* speak in Jesus' case of human nature as distinct from person, for it is the truth of his manhood from its very beginning and in the very nature of its conception. At the incarnation there never was conceived a human person, and in the nature of things *there never could have been,* because half—the male part—of the essential union simply did not exist in his case, any more than there existed that union itself without which a human person can have no being.

Yet the female part, the seed of the woman, did exist, and by divine creation therefrom the unique manhood of Jesus came into being. But from this *alone* it is crystal clear that no more than human *nature* can be predicated of that humanity; and equally clear, no less. Whence I conclude that, since the human nature of Jesus was created both solely and directly from the intact and singular seed of the woman by the Holy Ghost, then neither more nor less than true humanity was in that resultant moral and physical nature.

But Christ's humanity considered in and of itself alone in any event never had one moment of separate and distinct existence. With the creation by the Holy Ghost of that human nature as such, it was simultaneously and immediately taken into union at the incarnation of the Son of God. The Son straightway assumed his created humanity into union with his eternal divinity within the integrity of his own divine person. It was for the incarnation of the Son that this human nature was brought into existence by the Holy Ghost, and instantly the purpose of its being was realised and came to pass.

In this sense by the incarnation the person of the eternal Son added to himself and to his everlasting and innate divine nature, in that the full combination of properties essentially pertaining to manhood and giving to man distinctive human nature, was taken to be his own in the seed of the woman at conception. Thus whilst retaining in total integrity the whole of his unchanged divine nature in his own distinct person, he included—with that body in which he became incarnate—his new nature as man.

Furthermore, as a person the Son of God humbled himself amazingly in order to effect redemption for men. He became subject in and to the limitations of his new nature, as needing food, drink, warmth, shelter, comfort and companionship, as growing from infancy to childhood, boyhood to youth, and at last attaining full manhood. He was in manhood tempted in all points like as we are, yet without sin; he laboured and rested, slept and waked, walked and stood, ate and drank, spake and listened; he suffered and joyed, rejoiced and wept, he lived and died. In a word, he exhibited all the realities of human nature as man.

Yet withal the wonder of his divine nature could never be hid, and sometimes veritably glowed forth in full perfection! It is perfectly true that for the purpose of redemption he 'emptied himself', expressing himself in and through his human nature so as to be that true substitute of men: yet he never did so in such a way that there was the least vestige of diminishing or shadow of change in his divinity, or so as he was anything other than the one glorious person of the wonderful Son of God.

Then what do I understand by *person* as distinct from nature? By person I apprehend that which includes the whole of nature with all of nature's faculties and properties, but which does so by incorporating this whole as the vehicle of a distinct *self*. 'I live': not, I am a life, but strictly, distinct from my life, *I* live. 'I will': not, I am a will, but, separate from my will *I* am the one that wills. '*I* think', shows there is a distinct self-conscious *ego* for whom the mental faculties exist. A person therefore is inclusive of nature, but more, a person is the actual self of that man or woman whose nature it is.

A person then is that distinct, inviolate, integral, self-conscious identity to whom pertains separate self-conscious and aware being. This awareness is felt through nature, body and soul, but it is superior to that nature, being distinguished from it. Moreover a person is not dependent upon nature—of course apart from natural life itself—in order to be self-consciously aware. A person *is* that self-conscious *ego* in and of itself, and it is that centre of being out of which radiates the life natural to it, and from which the life permeates the whole of the wonderful and complex humanity, body and soul, proper to that distinct and separate person to whom it belongs.

Can *life* and person be distinguished then? In the doctrine of Christ, certainly. Jesus was possessed of human life as proper to his human nature, but he was not a human person: he was an eternal divine person possessed from the incarnation of human nature. Can life and person be distinguished with mankind in general? Yes they may be distinguished, and should be, but clearly they are coexistent, neither being able to subsist without the other.

It should be recalled that as to human nature I predicated two parts; the first was viewed as material and tangible, being that which pertained to the body. The second, belonging to the soul, was seen to be immaterial and intangible. As to the latter, this was divided between 'The essential properties of the soul in which the person gives expression to himself', and, 'The actual life of that soul'. Then, the life was regarded as belonging to the nature, but now it may be objected that I seem to associate it with the actual *person*.

But this is not really the case. The problem lies in the fact that though there is a necessity laid upon one to distinguish between things that differ, yet the different things flow and merge together into one harmonious whole. So that just as I distinguished between the function of the biochemical processes together with the delicate cellular structure of the brain and the highly sensitive physical apparatus of the nervous system, on the one hand: and, on the other, the more exterior functions of the immaterial soul in terms of the intelligence, the sensibility and the voluntary faculties: yet in fact at some point these things blend and flow together in one—so also at another and more interior point the central source of life in human nature merges with the person whose nature it is.

But one must distinguish: the *person* lives the life, the life lives neither the person nor itself. This being so, we may clearly say of the perfect humanity of Jesus Christ that whilst being possessed of all the qualities and attributes of human nature—including of necessity truly human life—neither in any way nor in any sense whatever could that humanity or that human life separately or together be referred to as person. On the contrary the person to whom this full and complete humanity belongs is the person of the eternal Son of God.

In view of the great importance of this distinction to the doctrine of Christ, then it follows that no matter what the difficulties encountered in mastering the differences between person and nature, and even in distinguishing between one part of nature from another, notwithstanding it is essential that one must persevere if one is rightly to come to the knowledge of Jesus the Son of God, and properly to honour his unique and glorious person. This is the very reason why I stress that there is an innate integrity of being and sovereignty of person distinct from and superior to nature as a whole, life included, whether in this world or passed on to the next, whether in the body or out of the body, whether in time or in eternity.

To equate person with nature is therefore false and damaging, quite preventing the apprehension of the truth; moreover it lays down a false premise which—because it touches the person of Christ—becomes frighteningly erroneous in the deviations which must always follow from all that is built upon a false basis. To put it another way: because of original corruption, pollution will always gush forth, for the spring itself has been poisonously contaminated at the very source.

I do not deny that from the very conception of mankind person and nature are indissolubly joined together: but two things may be joined together—or married—without their becoming the same thing, or losing their own distinct identity.

89

Moreover, when this present life is ended, and a person's body dies, that person still retains the immaterial attributes of the nature, even though the bodily and material parts of it corrupt and decay into dust: that is what is implied when referring to the immortal soul of a person. The intangible and immaterial qualities of human nature cannot be destroyed by the death of the body, they are carried *with the essential life* into the world to come, and are so carried *by the self-conscious being of the person* whose they are, and to whom they belong as inseparably joined world without end.

Indeed, when viewing the world to come it is even more clearly seen that there is an important difference not only between person and nature but also between the physical, material parts of nature and the moral immaterial parts: in a word, between what is mortal and what is immortal. One part survives death, the other does not. When death takes place the whole physical structure, the very body itself, ceases to function: it corrupts immediately, it decays and turns to dust.

But to conclude from the fact of death that the man himself therefore ceases to exist is ridiculous. As well might one conclude that man has no brain because it cannot be seen from the exterior. If it be replied, But it can be viewed by dissection. I answer, so also may be discerned by analysis the moral and spiritual parts of nature, and so equally well might be apprehended the person whose nature it is, from a little more penetration than may be obtained by the wilful and crass ignorance which supposes that man ceases with matter.

If it be granted that death is not more than the withdrawal of life from the mortal body and the consequent cessation of being from this present world, then one must conclude that the decay, corruption and subsequent mouldering away of the material and physical frame is all that is affected by death. The immaterial and intangible part of human nature is not affected, the moral and spiritual reality of humanity remains untouched, life itself is unaffected by its withdrawal from the corpse. Of this there are innumerable testimonies from the beginning of time up to this present moment.

But if this is true of the moral part of human nature itself, that in fact the intangible reality of the immortal soul lives on untouched by death, it is not affected, then *how much more* is it true of the vital, actual and real *person himself*, whose nature it is? Therefore if death—the death of the body and the separation of the soul therefrom—bears witness to the superiority of one part of human nature over the other part of it, how much more does is it demonstrate the transcendence of the *person* for whom the vehicle and medium of the whole human nature was brought into being, and for whom it was created to exist?

That fully aware and self-conscious persons retain after death all the faculties of their immortal souls has abundant testimony in Holy Scripture, just as it has witness in the first truths of inner consciousness. Moreover record is borne to this momentous truth by no small cloud of believing witnesses and that throughout all history. My reason for drawing attention to this fact here being in order to establish the superiority of the moral part of human nature over the physical, and the transcendence of the person over both.

Obviously this is exemplified if instances can be shown in which after the death of the body, the soul lived on fully possessed by the *ego*. And that is exactly what is illustrated in the messianic sixteenth psalm, where the body is seen as having been laid down in death: 'my flesh also shall rest in hope', and in confidence of its forthcoming resurrection: 'thou wilt not suffer thine Holy One to see corruption.' But what of the moral and spiritual part of nature after the death and burial of the body? 'Thou wilt not leave my *soul* in hell', shows the continued existence of the moral nature, or soul. As to the *person*, the fact that the psalmist says '*my* soul' declares that,

91

after death, separate from the body but present in the soul, he is *himself*, in person, in full possession of his *nature* as regards what is moral and intangible.

This truth is manifest in the case of Samuel. At the instigation of King Saul the woman with a familiar spirit who dwelt at En-dor brought up Samuel the prophet after he had died, in order to enquire of him concerning the future course that the King should be advised to take. The passage is a mysterious one, but there is no mystery about the plain declaration that it was Samuel's *person* that was brought up in spirit, nor in the fact that Samuel actually *felt* distress at this unlawful disturbance.

There can be few plainer passages showing the intangible part of human nature—the immortal soul—alive after the death of the body, than that to be seen in the sixth chapter of the book of the Revelation where John the divine saw 'the *souls* of them that *had been slain*.' And souls that possessed the conscious faculty of feeling, the awareness of hope, and a very strong sense of justice, for, 'They cried with a loud voice, saying, How long, O Lord, holy and true, dost thou not judge and avenge our blood on them that dwell on the earth?'

Before Lazarus was raised from the dead, his body had begun to corrupt; 'By this time he stinketh!' Now, if human nature depended upon the chemistry of the body for its existence and function, and if men were no more than physical beings, moreover if the person dissolved with death:—Where did he come from who came with *full faculties, memory, consciousness and all*, so to repossess the raised body of Lazarus? Because it could not and cannot be *seen* where he went with the *moral* part of his nature, it must not be supposed that he did not go! Indeed, Lazarus' *return* shows that there could be no question of his having continued his existence quite apart from his dead body and despite its corruption.

And of course this is equally true of the Shunammite's son; of him who revived when touched by the bones of Elisha; of the widow of Nain's son; of Jairus' daughter; of those 'women who received their dead raised to life again'; of the many saints that arose from the dead and appeared unto many in Jerusalem after the resurrection of the Lord Jesus, and of the great cloud of witnesses such as the *spirits* of just *men* made perfect!

Now I say that all this shows that not only is person superior to and distinct from nature, but that both are superior to death. The person whose nature it is, still retains and exercises both consciousness and personality through nature long after the body has died, decayed, and crumbled to dust. How else could Moses and Elias appear unto and talk intelligently with the Lord Jesus at the Mount of Transfiguration? They had been dead, physically, these thousands of years. He is—not *was*—the God of Abraham, of Isaac, and of Jacob, said Jesus, literally ages after the physical decease of these ancient patriarchs.

How otherwise could God *be* the God of Abraham, Isaac, and Jacob, unless the three patriarchs *were*, seeing God is not the God of the dead, but of the living? But their bodies were long dead. Then *they* retained their life independent of their dead bodies, untouched by time, age, decay, and death, and moreover they did so complete with all their moral faculties in the spiritual reality of their immortal souls. In a word, their *persons* retained their *distinctive moral nature*. It is certain that the Lord Jesus himself believed and taught this doctrine.

The parable of the rich man and Lazarus depends entirely for its meaning upon the facts now being presented. The present lifetime in the body is seen as being followed by a self-conscious awareness in the soul beyond the grave, where earthly injustices are fully set to rights and where the order that obtained in this world is turned upside down: 'Abraham' —after his physical death and burial, incidentally—'said, Son,

93

remember that thou in thy *lifetime* receivedst thy good things and likewise Lazarus evil things: but *now* he is comforted and thou art tormented.' Here is glimpsed a world after death in which sensibly aware persons possessed of all their moral faculties are made to feel and experience the consequences of the judgment of God upon their erstwhile worldly existence, voluntary action, and obligations in that past lifetime before the grave, and once spent in the body.

Several other references—above all the case of Jesus himself during the period between his death and resurrection: not to mention the forty days after it!—might be brought forward with profit to establish further this present argument. However, it is not now my object to present every possible instance of self-conscious awareness after death, nor is it to assert the general resurrection of the dead, as bearing upon the truth under consideration.

My present object is to point out from a sufficient number of references that, firstly, the moral part of human nature functions independently after the death and decay of the physical; and secondly, that the self-conscious person whose nature it is—and who is by definition superior to and distinct from that nature—is fully possessed and clearly aware of the intangible and immaterial faculties of the immortal soul not only in this life but also long after the corruption and decay of the body.

The reason for this argument—and the object in view in bringing forward these truths revealed from glimpses of the life and world to come—being to clarify still further the difference between nature and person by drawing attention to the distinctions drawn in, by, and after death.

By this means it will become increasingly apparent as to why it is essential to stress that the Son of God was not a human *person* but a divine person who had assumed human *nature* into union with his divine nature at the incarnation; moreover to stress what is meant by his human nature and divine person respectively; and finally, to show precisely wherein lies the actual and vital distinction between the two relevant terms.

For one's constant aim—in expounding the operation of the Holy Ghost at the incarnation—has been to clarify and uphold the doctrine that it was human nature, neither more nor less, in both body and soul, that the Holy Ghost created from the seed of the woman for the incarnation and assumption of the divine person of the eternal Son, who brought forthwith that humanity into union with his own everlasting and unchanged nature as God.

I say, the creation of this perfect humanity from Mary's seed was the separate and singular work of the Holy Ghost. And wonderfully profound and richly complex as is the unique manhood thus formed, notwithstanding, we are not under any circumstances to confuse its rich, perfect, and profound combination of properties or essential qualities with *person*.

Human *nature* is the *vehicle* for the *human expression* of a person, and the human nature of the Son of God is the *only* human nature that is not the vehicle and expression of a *human* person. It is, I say, the unique vehicle and singular expression of the *divine* person of the Son of God, who was— it goes without saying—immutably and everlastingly possessed of and expressed in his own intrinsic divine nature. From the incarnation, to effect redemption and to bring in the eternal purpose of God in the world to come, the person of the Son was and is now manifested in that human nature which he has taken into perpetual union with himself.

Hence we may say that he is a real man: behold how profound and rich is that perfect humanity, physical and moral nature, taken by the Holy Ghost from the seed of David, the seed of Abraham. He has true human nature; he is possessed of real human life; his is perfect manhood: nothing less was created by the Holy Ghost from the seed of the virgin Mary.

By observing correctly the work of the Holy Spirit at the incarnation, we are enabled to honour the Son, to magnify the mystery of Christ, and to glorify his holy name. Wherefore? Because we have been led rightly to discern his wonderful person, to worship his awesome divinity, and to observe his perfect humanity.

Thus it is that a view of the operation of the Holy Ghost is certainly required properly to know the person of Jesus the Son of God. Such a discerning insight into the gospel of Christ opens the heart to look upon that superlative and glorious person of the Son—'Believe on the Lord Jesus Christ, and thou shalt be saved, and thy house'—as it does to see aright the work and thence gladly to worship the being of God in three persons: Father, Son, and Holy Ghost, to whom be the glory, world without end. Amen.

Now to him that is of power to stablish you according to my gospel, and the preaching of Jesus Christ, according to the revelation of the mystery, which was kept secret since the world began, but now is manifest, and by the scriptures of the prophets, according to the commandment of the everlasting God, made known to all nations for the obedience of faith: To God only wise, be glory through Jesus Christ for ever. Amen.

JOHN METCALFE

INDEX

TO OTHER PUBLICATIONS

PSALMS, HYMNS AND SPIRITUAL SONGS

THE PSALMS

OF THE

OLD TESTAMENT

The Psalms of the Old Testament, the result of years of painstaking labour, is an original translation into verse from the Authorised Version, which seeks to present the Psalms in the purest scriptural form possible for singing. Here, for the first time, divine names are rendered as and when they occur in the scripture, the distinction between LORD and Lord has been preserved, and every essential point of doctrine and experience appears with unique perception and fidelity.

The Psalms of the Old Testament is the first part of a trilogy written by John Metcalfe, the second part of which is entitled *Spiritual Songs from the Gospels*, and the last, *The Hymns of the New Testament*. These titles provide unique and accurate metrical versions of passages from the psalms, the gospels and the new testament epistles respectively, and are intended to be used together in the worship of God.

Price £2.50 *(postage extra)*
(hard-case binding, dust-jacket)
Printed, sewn and bound
by the John Metcalfe Publishing Trust
ISBN 0 9506366 7 3

SPIRITUAL SONGS

FROM

THE GOSPELS

The *Spiritual Songs from the Gospels*, the result of years of painstaking labour, is an original translation into verse from the Authorised Version, which seeks to present essential parts of the gospels in the purest scriptural form possible for singing. The careful selection from Matthew, Mark, Luke and John, set forth in metrical verse of the highest integrity, enables the singer to sing 'the word of Christ' as if from the scripture itself, 'richly and in all wisdom'; and, above all, in a way that facilitates worship in song of unprecedented fidelity.

The *Spiritual Songs from the Gospels* is the central part of a trilogy written by John Metcalfe, the first part of which is entitled *The Psalms of the Old Testament*, and the last, *The Hymns of the New Testament*. These titles provide unique and accurate metrical versions of passages from the psalms, the gospels and the new testament epistles respectively, and are intended to be used together in the worship of God.

Price £2.50 *(postage extra)*
(hard-case binding, dust-jacket)
Printed, sewn and bound
by the John Metcalfe Publishing Trust
ISBN 0 9506366 8 1

THE HYMNS

OF THE

NEW TESTAMENT

The *Hymns of the New Testament*, the result of years of painstaking labour, is an original translation into verse from the Authorised Version, which presents essential parts of the new testament epistles in the purest scriptural form possible for singing. The careful selection from the book of Acts to that of Revelation, set forth in metrical verse of the highest integrity, enables the singer to sing 'the word of Christ' as if from the scripture itself, 'richly and in all wisdom'; and, above all, in a way that facilitates worship in song of unprecedented fidelity.

The *Hymns of the New Testament* is the last part of a trilogy written by John Metcalfe, the first part of which is entitled *The Psalms of the Old Testament*, and the next, *Spiritual Songs from the Gospels*. These titles provide unique and accurate metrical versions of passages from the psalms, the gospels and the new testament epistles respectively, and are intended to be used together in the worship of God.

Price £2.50 *(postage extra)*
(hard-case binding, dust-jacket)
Printed, sewn and bound
by the John Metcalfe Publishing Trust
ISBN 0 9506366 9 X

'THE APOSTOLIC FOUNDATION OF THE CHRISTIAN CHURCH' SERIES

NEWLY REPUBLISHED

FOUNDATIONS UNCOVERED

THE APOSTOLIC FOUNDATION
OF THE
CHRISTIAN CHURCH

Volume I

Foundations Uncovered is a small book of some 41 pages. This is the introduction to the major series: 'The Apostolic Foundation of the Christian Church'.

Rich in truth, the Introduction deals comprehensively with the foundation of the apostolic faith under the descriptive titles: The Word, The Doctrine, The Truth, The Gospel, The Faith, The New Testament, and The Foundation.

The contents of the book reveal: The Fact of the Foundation; The Foundation Uncovered; What the Foundation is not; How the Foundation is Described; and, Being Built upon the Foundation.

'This book comes with the freshness of a new Reformation.'

Price 30p *(postage extra)*
(Laminated cover)
Printed, sewn and bound
by the John Metcalfe Publishing Trust
ISBN 0 9506366 5 7

To meet constant and world-wide demand
for this 'Truly great Christian work'
since selling out the entire stock
of all previous printings, the Trust
is glad to announce a completely new
1993 second edition, thoroughly revised

THE BIRTH OF JESUS CHRIST

THE APOSTOLIC FOUNDATION
OF THE
CHRISTIAN CHURCH

Volume II

'The very spirit of adoration and worship rings through the pages of *The Birth of Jesus Christ*.

'The author expresses with great clarity the truths revealed to him in his study of holy scriptures at depth. We are presented here with a totally lofty view of the Incarnation.

'John Metcalfe is to be classed amongst the foremost expositors of our age; and his writings have about them that quality of timelessness that makes me sure they will one day take their place among the heritage of truly great Christian works.'

From a review by Rev. David Catterson.

'Uncompromisingly faithful to scripture ... has much to offer which is worth serious consideration ... deeply moving.'

The Expository Times.

Price 95p *(postage extra)*
(Laminated Cover)
Printed, sewn and bound
by the John Metcalfe Publishing Trust
ISBN 1 870039 48 3

THE MESSIAH

THE APOSTOLIC FOUNDATION
OF THE
CHRISTIAN CHURCH

Volume III

The Messiah is a spiritually penetrating and entirely original exposition of Matthew chapter one to chapter seven from the trenchant pen of John Metcalfe.

Matthew Chapters One to Seven

GENEALOGY · BIRTH · STAR OF BETHLEHEM
HEROD · FLIGHT TO EGYPT · NAZARETH
JOHN THE BAPTIST · THE BAPTIST'S MINISTRY
JESUS' BAPTISM · ALL RIGHTEOUSNESS FULFILLED
HEAVEN OPENED · THE SPIRIT'S DESCENT
THE TEMPTATION OF JESUS IN THE WILDERNESS
JESUS' MANIFESTATION · THE CALLING · THE TRUE DISCIPLES
THE BEATITUDES · THE SERMON ON THE MOUNT

'Something of the fire of the ancient Hebrew prophet .... Metcalfe has spiritual and expository potentials of a high order.'

The Life of Faith.

Price £2.45 *(postage extra)*
(425 pages, Laminated Cover)
ISBN 0 9502515 8 5

THE SON OF GOD AND SEED OF DAVID

THE APOSTOLIC FOUNDATION
OF THE
CHRISTIAN CHURCH

Volume IV

The Son of God and Seed of David is the fourth volume in the major work entitled 'The Apostolic Foundation of the Christian Church.'

'The author proceeds to open and allege that Jesus Christ is and ever was *The Son of God*. This greatest of subjects, this most profound of all mysteries, is handled with reverence and with outstanding perception.

'The second part considers *The Seed of David*. What is meant precisely by 'the seed'? And why 'of David'? With prophetic insight the author expounds these essential verities.'

Price £6.95 *(postage extra)*
Hardback 250 pages
Laminated bookjacket
Printed, sewn and bound
by the John Metcalfe Publishing Trust
ISBN 1 870039 16 5

CHRIST CRUCIFIED

THE APOSTOLIC FOUNDATION
OF THE
CHRISTIAN CHURCH

Volume V

Christ Crucified the definitive work on the crucifixion, the blood, and the cross of Jesus Christ.

The crucifixion of Jesus Christ witnessed in the Gospels: the gospel according to Matthew; Mark; Luke; John.

The blood of Jesus Christ declared in the Epistles: the shed blood; the blood of purchase; redemption through his blood; the blood of sprinkling; the blood of the covenant.

The doctrine of the cross revealed in the apostolic foundation of the Christian church: the doctrine of the cross; the cross and the body of sin; the cross and the carnal mind; the cross and the law; the offence of the cross; the cross of our Lord Jesus Christ.

Price £6.95 *(postage extra)*
Hardback 300 pages
Laminated bookjacket
Printed, sewn and bound
by the John Metcalfe Publishing Trust
ISBN 1 870039 08 4

JUSTIFICATION BY FAITH

THE APOSTOLIC FOUNDATION
OF THE
CHRISTIAN CHURCH

Volume VI

THE HEART OF THE GOSPEL · THE FOUNDATION OF THE CHURCH
THE ISSUE OF ETERNITY
CLEARLY, ORIGINALLY AND POWERFULLY OPENED

The basis · The righteousness of the law
The righteousness of God · The atonement · Justification
Traditional views considered · Righteousness imputed to faith
Faith counted for righteousness · Justification by Faith

'And it came to pass, when Jesus had ended these sayings, the people were astonished at his doctrine: for he taught them as one having authority, and not as the scribes.' Matthew 7:28,29.

Price £7.50 *(postage extra)*
Hardback 375 pages
Laminated bookjacket
Printed, sewn and bound
by the John Metcalfe Publishing Trust
ISBN 1870039 11 4

THE CHURCH: WHAT IS IT?

THE APOSTOLIC FOUNDATION
OF THE
CHRISTIAN CHURCH

Volume VII

The answer to this question proceeds first from the lips of Jesus himself, Mt. 16:18, later to be expounded by the words of the apostles whom he sent.

Neither fear of man nor favour from the world remotely affect the answer.

Here is the truth, the whole truth, and nothing but the truth.

The complete originality, the vast range, and the total fearlessness of this book command the attention in a way that is unique.

Read this book: you will never read another like it.

Outspokenly devastating yet devastatingly constructive.

Price £7.75 (postage extra)
Hardback 400 pages
Laminated bookjacket
Printed, sewn and bound
by the John Metcalfe Publishing Trust
ISBN 1 870039 23 8

OTHER TITLES

NOAH AND THE FLOOD

Noah and the Flood expounds with vital urgency the man and the message that heralded the end of the old world. The description of the flood itself is vividly realistic. The whole work has an unmistakable ring of authority, and speaks as 'Thus saith the Lord'.

'Mr. Metcalfe makes a skilful use of persuasive eloquence as he challenges the reality of one's profession of faith ... he gives a rousing call to a searching self-examination and evaluation of one's spiritual experience.'

The Monthly Record of the Free Church of Scotland.

Price £1.90 *(postage extra)*
(Laminated Cover)
Printed, sewn and bound
by the John Metcalfe Publishing Trust
ISBN 1 870039 22 X

DIVINE FOOTSTEPS

Divine Footsteps traces the pathway of the feet of the Son of man from the very beginning in the prophetic figures of the true in the old testament through the reality in the new; doing so in a way of experimental spirituality. At the last a glimpse of the coming glory is beheld as his feet are viewed as standing at the latter day upon the earth.

Price 95p *(postage extra)*
(Laminated Cover)
Printed, sewn and bound
by the John Metcalfe Publishing Trust
ISBN 1 870039 21 1

THE RED HEIFER

The Red Heifer was the name given to a sacrifice used by the children of Israel in the Old Testament—as recorded in Numbers 19—in which a heifer was slain and burned. Cedar wood, hyssop and scarlet were cast into the burning, and the ashes were mingled with running water and put in a vessel. It was kept for the children of Israel for a water of separation: it was a purification for sin.

In this unusual book the sacrifice is brought up to date and its relevance to the church today is shown.

Price 75p *(postage extra)*
ISBN 0 9502515 4 2

THE WELLS OF SALVATION

The Wells of Salvation is written from a series of seven powerful addresses preached at Tylers Green. It is a forthright and experimental exposition of Isaiah 12:3, 'Therefore with joy shall ye draw water out of the wells of salvation.'

John Metcalfe is acknowledged to be perhaps the most gifted expositor and powerful preacher of our day and this is to be seen clearly in The Wells of Salvation.

Price £1.50 *(postage extra)*
(Laminated Cover)
ISBN 0 9502515 6 9

OF GOD OR MAN?

LIGHT FROM GALATIANS

The Epistle to the Galatians contends for deliverance from the law and from carnal ministry.

The Apostle opens his matter in two ways:

Firstly, Paul vindicates himself and his ministry against those that came not from God above, but from Jerusalem below.

Secondly, he defends the Gospel and evangelical liberty against legal perversions and bondage to the flesh.

Price £1.45 (postage extra)
(Laminated Cover)
ISBN 0 9506366 3 0

A QUESTION FOR POPE JOHN PAUL II

As a consequence of his many years spent apart in prayer, lonely vigil, and painstaking study of the scripture, John Metcalfe asks a question and looks for an answer from Pope John Paul II.

Price £1.25. (postage extra)
(Laminated Cover)
ISBN 0 9506366 4 9

THE BOOK OF RUTH

The Book of Ruth is set against the farming background of old testament Israel at the time of the Judges, the narrative—unfolding the work of God in redemption—being marked by a series of agricultural events.

These events—the famine; the barley harvest; the wheat harvest; the winnowing—possessed a hidden spiritual significance to that community, but, much more, they speak in figure directly to our own times, as the book reveals.

Equally contemporary appear the characters of Ruth, Naomi, Boaz, and the first kinsman, drawn with spiritual perception greatly to the profit of the reader.

Price £4.95 *(postage extra)*
Hardback 200 pages
Laminated bookjacket
Printed, sewn and bound
by the John Metcalfe Publishing Trust
ISBN 1 870039 17 3

PRESENT-DAY CONVERSIONS
OF THE NEW TESTAMENT KIND

FROM THE MINISTRY OF

JOHN METCALFE

The outstandingly striking presentation of this fascinating paperback will surely catch the eye, as its title and contents will certainly captivate the mind: here is a unique publication.

Woven into a gripping narrative, over twenty-one short life stories, all centred on conversions that simply could not have happened had not God broken in, and had not Christ been revealed, the book presents a tremendous challenge, at once moving and thrilling to the reader.

Price £2.25 *(postage extra)*
(Laminated Cover)
Printed, sewn and bound
by the John Metcalfe Publishing Trust
ISBN 1 870039 31 9

DIVINE MEDITATIONS

OF

WILLIAM HUNTINGTON

Originally published by Mr. Huntington as a series of letters to J. Jenkins, under the title of 'Contemplations on the God of Israel', the spiritual content of this correspondence has been skilfully and sympathetically edited, abridged, and arranged so as to form a series of meditations, suitable for daily readings.

Mr. Huntington's own text is thereby adapted to speak directly to the reader in a way much more suited to his ministering immediately to ourselves, in our own circumstances and times.

It is greatly hoped that many today will benefit from this adaption which carefully retains both the spirit and the letter of the text. If any prefer the original format, this is readily available from several sources and many libraries.

Nevertheless, the publishers believe the much more readable form into which Mr. Huntington's very words have been adapted will appeal to a far wider audience, for whose comfort and consolation this carefully edited work has been published.

Price £2.35 (*postage extra*)
(Laminated Cover)
Printed, sewn and bound
by the John Metcalfe Publishing Trust
ISBN 1 870039 24 6

SAVING FAITH

The sevenfold work of the Holy Ghost in bringing a sinner to saving faith in Christ opened and enlarged.

True faith is the work of God. False faith is the presumption of man. But where is the difference? *Saving Faith* shows the difference.

Price £2.25 *(postage extra)*
Paperback 250 pages
(Laminated Cover)
Printed, sewn and bound
by the John Metcalfe Publishing Trust
ISBN 1 870039 40 8

DELIVERANCE FROM THE LAW
THE WESTMINSTER CONFESSION EXPLODED

Deliverance from the law. A devastating vindication of the gospel of Christ against the traditions of man.

Price £1.90 *(postage extra)*
Paperback 160 pages
(Laminated Cover)
Printed, sewn and bound
by the John Metcalfe Publishing Trust
ISBN 1 870039 41 6

NEWLY PUBLISHED

THE BEATITUDES

A unique insight destined to be the classic opening of this
wonderful sequence of utterances from the lips of Jesus.

The reader will discover a penetration of the spiritual heights
and divine depths of these peerless words in a way ever fresh
and always rewarding though read time and time again.

Price £1.90 *(postage extra)*
Paperback 185 pages
(Laminated cover)
Printed, sewn and bound
by the John Metcalfe Publishing Trust
ISBN 1 870039 45 9

'TRACT FOR THE TIMES' SERIES

xxx

THE GOSPEL OF GOD

'TRACT FOR THE TIMES' SERIES

The Gospel of God. Beautifully designed, this tract positively describes the gospel under the following headings: The Gospel is of God; The Gospel is Entirely of God; The Gospel is Entire in Itself; The Gospel is Preached; The Gospel Imparts Christ; and, Nothing But the Gospel Imparts Christ.

Price 25p *(postage extra)*
(Laminated Cover)
No. 1 in the Series

THE STRAIT GATE

'TRACT FOR THE TIMES' SERIES

The Strait Gate. Exceptionally well made, this booklet consists of extracts from 'The Messiah', compiled in such a way as to challenge the shallowness of much of today's 'easy-believism', whilst positively pointing to the strait gate.

Price 25p *(postage extra)*
(Laminated Cover)
No. 2 in the Series

ETERNAL SONSHIP
AND TAYLOR BRETHREN

'TRACT FOR THE TIMES' SERIES

Eternal Sonship and Taylor Brethren. This booklet is highly recommended, particularly for those perplexed by James Taylor's teaching against the eternal sonship of Christ.

Price 25p *(postage extra)*
(Laminated Cover)
No. 3 in the Series

MARKS OF THE
NEW TESTAMENT CHURCH

Marks of the New Testament Church. This exposition from Acts 2:42 declares what were, and what were not, the abiding marks of the church. The apostles' doctrine, fellowship and ordinances are lucidly explained.

Price 25p *(postage extra)*
(Laminated Cover)
No. 4 in the Series

THE CHARISMATIC DELUSION

The Charismatic Delusion. A prophetic message revealing the fundamental error of this movement which has swept away so many in the tide of its popularity. Here the delusion is dispelled.

Price 25p *(postage extra)*
(Laminated Cover)
No. 5 in the Series

PREMILLENNIALISM EXPOSED

Premillennialism Exposed. Well received evangelically, particularly through the influence of J.N. Darby, the Schofield bible, and the Plymouth Brethren, Premillennialism has assumed the cloak of orthodoxy. In this tract the cloak is removed, and the unorthodoxy of this system is exposed. A remarkable revelation.

Price 25p *(postage extra)*
(Laminated Cover)
No. 6 in the Series

JUSTIFICATION AND PEACE

'TRACT FOR THE TIMES' SERIES

Justification and Peace. This tract is taken from a message preached in December 1984 at Penang Hill, Malaysia. In this well-known address, peace with God is seen to be based upon nothing save justification by faith. No one should miss this tract.

Price 25p *(postage extra)*
(Laminated Cover)
No. 7 in the Series

FAITH OR PRESUMPTION?

'TRACT FOR THE TIMES' SERIES

Faith or presumption? The eighth tract in this vital series exposes the difference between faith and presumption, showing that faith is not of the law, neither is is apart from the work of God, nor is it of man. The work of God in man that precedes saving faith is opened generally and particularly, and the tract goes on to reveal positively the nature of saving faith. Belief and 'easy-believism' are contrasted, making clear the difference between the two, as the system of presumption—called easy-believism—is clearly shown, and the way of true belief pointed out with lucid clarity.

Price 25p *(postage extra)*
(Laminated Cover)
No. 8 in the Series

THE ELECT UNDECEIVED
'TRACT FOR THE TIMES' SERIES

The Elect undeceived, the ninth Tract for the Times, earnestly contends for 'the faith once delivered to the saints' in a way that is spiritually edifying, positive, and subject to the Lord Jesus Christ according to the scriptures.

The Tract is a response to the pamphlet 'Salvation and the Church' published jointly by the Catholic Truth Society and Church House Publishing, in which the Anglican and Roman Catholic Commissioners agree together about JUSTIFICATION. The pamphlet shows how they have agreed.

Price 25p *(postage extra)*
(Laminated Cover)
No. 9 in the Series

JUSTIFYING RIGHTEOUSNESS
'TRACT FOR THE TIMES' SERIES

Justifying Righteousness. Was it wrought by the law of Moses or by the blood of Christ? Written not in the language of dead theology but that of the living God, here is the vital and experimental doctrine of the new testament. Part of the book 'Justification by Faith', nevertheless this tract has a message in itself essential to those who would know and understand the truth.

Price 25p *(postage extra)*
(Laminated Cover)
No. 10 in the Series

RIGHTEOUSNESS IMPUTED
'TRACT FOR THE TIMES' SERIES

Righteousness Imputed. The truth of the gospel and the fallacy of tradition. Here the gospel trumpet of the jubilee is sounded in no uncertain terms, as on the one hand that truth essential to be believed for salvation is opened from holy scripture, and on the other the errors of Brethrenism are brought to light in a unique and enlightening way. This tract is taken from the book 'Justification by Faith', but in itself it conveys a message of great penetration and clarity.

Price 25p *(postage extra)*
(Laminated Cover)
No. 11 in the Series

THE GREAT DECEPTION
'TRACT FOR THE TIMES' SERIES

The Great Deception. The erosion of Justification by faith. All ministers, every Christian, and each assembly ought not only to possess but to read and reread this prophetic message as the word of the Lord to this generation, set in the context of the age. This tract is part of the book 'Justification by Faith' but contains within itself a message which is at once vital and authoritative.

Price 25p *(postage extra)*
(Laminated Cover)
No. 12 in the Series

A FAMINE IN THE LAND

'TRACT FOR THE TIMES' SERIES

A Famine in the Land. Taken from the Book of Ruth, with telling forcefulness this tract opens conditions exactly parallel to those of our own times. 'Behold, the days come, saith the Lord GOD, that I will send a famine in the land, not a famine of bread, nor a thirst for water, but of hearing the words of the LORD: and they shall wander from sea to sea, and from the north even to the east, they shall run to and fro to seek the word of the LORD, and shall not find it.'

Price 25p *(postage extra)*
(Laminated Cover)
No. 13 in the Series

BLOOD AND WATER

'TRACT FOR THE TIMES' SERIES

Blood and Water. Of the four gospels, only John reveals the truth that blood was shed at the cross. When it was shed, Jesus was dead already. With the blood there came forth water. But what do these things mean? With devastating present-day application, this tract tells you what they mean.

Price 25p *(postage extra)*
(Laminated Cover)
No. 14 in the Series

WOMEN BISHOPS?

'TRACT FOR THE TIMES' SERIES

Women Bishops? This is a question that has arisen in America, but should it have arisen at all?
Read this tract and find out the authoritative answer.

Price 25p *(postage extra)*
(Laminated Cover)
No. 15 in the Series

THE HEAVENLY VISION

'TRACT FOR THE TIMES' SERIES

The Heavenly Vision not only transformed the prophet himself, it became a savour of life unto life—or death unto death—to all the people.
'*Where there is no vision the people perish*', Proverbs 29:18. This is true. But where is the vision today? And what is the vision today? This tract answers those questions.

Price 25p *(Postage extra)*
(Laminated Cover)
No. 16 in the Series

EVANGELICAL TRACTS

EVANGELICAL TRACTS

1. **The Two Prayers of Elijah.** Green card cover, price 10p.

2. **Wounded for our Transgressions.** Gold card cover, price 10p.

3. **The Blood of Sprinkling.** Red card cover, price 10p.

4. **The Grace of God that brings Salvation.** Blue card cover, price 10p.

5. **The Name of Jesus.** Rose card cover, price 10p.

6. **The Ministry of the New Testament.** Purple card cover, price 10p.

7. **The Death of the Righteous** (*The closing days of J.B. Stoney*) by A.M.S. (his daughter). Ivory card cover, Price 10p.

8. **Repentance.** Sky blue card cover, price 10p.

9. **Legal Deceivers Exposed.** Crimson card cover, price 10p.

10. **Unconditional Salvation.** Green card cover, price 10p.

11. **Religious Merchandise.** Brown card cover, price 10p.

ECCLESIA TRACTS

ECCLESIA TRACTS

The Beginning of the Ecclesia by John Metcalfe. No. 1 in the Series, Sand grain cover, Price 10p.

Churches and the Church by J.N. Darby. Edited. No. 2 in the Series, Sand grain cover, Price 10p.

The Ministers of Christ by John Metcalfe. No. 3 in the Series, Sand grain cover, Price 10p.

The Inward Witness by George Fox. Edited. No. 4 in the Series, Sand grain cover, Price 10p.

The Notion of a Clergyman by J.N. Darby. Edited. No. 5 in the Series, Sand grain cover, Price 10p.

The Servant of the Lord by William Huntington. Edited and Abridged. No. 6 in the Series, Sand grain cover, Price 10p.

One Spirit by William Kelly. Edited. No. 7 in the Series, Sand grain cover, Price 10p.

The Funeral of Arminianism by William Huntington. Edited and Abridged. No. 8 in the Series, Sand grain cover, Price 10p.

One Body by William Kelly. Edited. No. 9 in the Series, Sand grain cover, Price 10p.

False Churches and True by John Metcalfe. No. 10 in the Series, Sand grain cover, Price 10p.

Separation from Evil by J.N. Darby. Edited. No. 11 in the Series, Sand grain cover, Price 10p.

The Remnant by J.B. Stoney. Edited. No. 12 in the Series, Sand grain cover, Price 10p.

The Arminian Skeleton by William Huntington. Edited and Abridged. No. 13 in the Series, Sand grain cover, Price 10p.

MINISTRY BY JOHN METCALFE

TAPE MINISTRY BY JOHN METCALFE
FROM ENGLAND AND THE FAR EAST
IS AVAILABLE.

In order to obtain this free recorded ministry, please send your blank cassette (C.90) and the cost of the return postage, including your name and address in block capitals, to the John Metcalfe Publishing Trust, Church Road, Tylers Green, Penn, Bucks, HP10 8LN. Tapelists are available on request.

Owing to the increased demand for the tape ministry, we are unable to supply more than two tapes per order, except in the case of meetings for the hearing of tapes, where a special arrangement can be made.

THE MINISTRY OF THE NEW TESTAMENT

The purpose of this substantial A4 gloss paper magazine is to provide spiritual and experimental ministry with sound doctrine which rightly and prophetically divides the Word of Truth.

Readers of our books will already know the high standards of our publications. They can be confident that these pages will maintain that quality, by giving access to enduring ministry from the past, much of which is derived from sources that are virtually unobtainable today, and publishing a living ministry from the present. Selected articles from the following writers have already been included:

ELI ASHDOWN · ABRAHAM BOOTH · JOHN BUNYAN · JOHN BURGON
JOHN CALVIN · DONALD CARGILL · JOHN CENNICK
J.N. DARBY · GEORGE FOX · JOHN FOXE · WILLIAM GADSBY
GREY HAZLERIGG · WILLIAM HUNTINGTON · WILLIAM KELLY
JOHN KENNEDY · JOHN KERSHAW · HANSERD KNOLLYS
JAMES LEWIS · MARTIN LUTHER · ROBERT MURRAY MCCHEYNE
JOHN METCALFE · ALEXANDER—SANDY—PEDEN · J.C. PHILPOT
J.K. POPHAM · JAMES RENWICK · J.B. STONEY · HENRY TANNER
ARTHUR TRIGGS · JOHN VINALL · JOHN WARBURTON
JOHN WELWOOD · GEORGE WHITEFIELD · J.A. WYLIE

Price £1.75 *(postage included)*
Issued Spring, Summer, Autumn, Winter.

Book Order Form

Please send to the address below:-

	Price	Quantity
A Question for Pope John Paul II	£1.25	......
Of God or Man?	£1.45	......
Noah and the Flood	£1.90	......
Divine Footsteps	£0.95	......
The Red Heifer	£0.75	......
The Wells of Salvation	£1.50	......
The Book of Ruth (Hardback edition)	£4.95	......
Divine Meditations of William Huntington	£2.35	......
Present-Day Conversions of the New Testament Kind	£2.25	......
Saving Faith	£2.25	......
Deliverance from the Law	£1.90	......
The Beatitudes	£1.90	......

Psalms, Hymns & Spiritual Songs (Hardback edition)

	Price	Quantity
The Psalms of the Old Testament	£2.50	......
Spiritual Songs from the Gospels	£2.50	......
The Hymns of the New Testament	£2.50	......

'Apostolic Foundation of the Christian Church' series

		Price	Quantity
Foundations Uncovered	Vol.I	£0.30	......
The Birth of Jesus Christ	Vol.II	£0.95	......
The Messiah	Vol.III	£2.45	......
The Son of God and Seed of David (Hardback edition)	Vol.IV	£6.95	......
Christ Crucified (Hardback edition)	Vol.V	£6.95	......
Justification by Faith (Hardback edition)	Vol.VI	£7.50	......
The Church: What is it? (Hardback edition)	Vol.VII	£7.75	......

Name and Address (in block capitals)

. . . .

. . . .

. . . .

If money is sent with order please allow for postage. Please address to:- The John Metcalfe Publishing Trust, Church Road, Tylers Green, Penn, Bucks, HP10 8LN.

cut here

Tract Order Form

Please send to the address below:-

		Price	Quantity
Evangelical Tracts			
The Two Prayers of Elijah		£0.10	......
Wounded for our Transgressions		£0.10	......
The Blood of Sprinkling		£0.10	......
The Grace of God that Brings Salvation		£0.10	......
The Name of Jesus		£0.10	......
The Ministry of the New Testament		£0.10	......
The Death of the Righteous by A.M.S.		£0.10	......
Repentance		£0.10	......
Legal Deceivers Exposed		£0.10	......
Unconditional Salvation		£0.10	......
Religious Merchandise		£0.10	......
'Tract for the Times' series			
The Gospel of God	No.1	£0.25	......
The Strait Gate	No.2	£0.25	......
Eternal Sonship and Taylor Brethren	No.3	£0.25	......
Marks of the New Testament Church	No.4	£0.25	......
The Charismatic Delusion	No.5	£0.25	......
Premillennialism Exposed	No.6	£0.25	......
Justification and Peace	No.7	£0.25	......
Faith or presumption?	No.8	£0.25	......
The Elect undeceived	No.9	£0.25	......
Justifying Righteousness	No.10	£0.25	......
Righteousness Imputed	No.11	£0.25	......
The Great Deception	No.12	£0.25	......
A Famine in the Land	No.13	£0.25	......
Blood and Water	No.14	£0.25	......
Women Bishops?	No.15	£0.25	......
The Heavenly Vision	No.16	£0.25	
Ecclesia Tracts			
The Beginning of the Ecclesia	No.1	£0.10	......
Churches and the Church (J.N.D.)	No.2	£0.10	......
The Ministers of Christ	No.3	£0.10	......
The Inward Witness (G.F.)	No.4	£0.10	......
The Notion of a Clergyman (J.N.D.)	No.5	£0.10	......
The Servant of the Lord (W.H.)	No.6	£0.10	......
One Spirit (W.K.)	No.7	£0.10	......
The Funeral of Arminianism (W.H.)	No.8	£0.10	......
One Body (W.K.)	No.9	£0.10	......
False Churches and True	No.10	£0.10	......
Separation from Evil (J.N.D.)	No.11	£0.10	......
The Remnant (J.B.S.)	No.12	£0.10	......
The Arminian Skeleton (W.H.)	No.13	£0.10	

Name and Address (in block capitals)

. . . .

. . . .

. . . .

If money is sent with order please allow for postage. Please address to:- The
John Metcalfe Publishing Trust, Church Road, Tylers Green, Penn, Bucks, HP10 8LN.

cut here